THE BUGBEAR OF LITERACY

"Progress," by Eric Gill

THE BUGBEAR
OF
LITERACY

ANANDA K. COOMARASWAMY

With an Introduction by
Robert Allerton Parker

Angelico Press

For information, address:
Angelico Press, Ltd.
169 Monitor St.
Brooklyn, NY 11222
www.angelicopress.com

paper 978-1-62138-768-8
cloth 978-1-62138-769-5

Cover design by
Michael Schrauzer

CONTENTS

INTRODUCTION

DR. COOMARASWAMY has been living and writing in the United States for the past thirty years, but the fruits of his mature thought have never before been made easily accessible to the intelligent layman. To remedy this lack, we have collected these representative essays, which throw so searching a light upon the problems of the present crisis of the human race. To certain readers, Coomaraswamy's ideas may seem highly controversial and destructive of commonly accepted assumptions. Such antagonists may object that this indictment of modern Western civilization is based upon obstinate age-old Oriental prejudices. But Ananda Coomaraswamy is not merely "an eminent Orientalist" (as Aldous Huxley characterizes him in *The Perennial Philosophy*); nor is he merely an authority on Oriental art. The ideas he formulates in these essays and reviews are expressed with the authority of a lifetime of scholarship. He writes, as he has elsewhere explained, "from a strictly orthodox point of view . . . endeavoring to speak with mathematical precision, but never employing words of our own, or making any affirmations for which authority could not be cited by chapter and verse; in this way making even our technique characteristically Indian."

Since Dr. Coomaraswamy deprecates personality and personalism, and condemns the contemporary mania for exhibitionary self-exploitation, he is the most reticent of men in furnishing biographical details. Yet, for lay readers, such details, and an outline of his crowded career, seem necessary for an understanding of the broad foundations of his thought. It may come as a surprise, for instance, to know that his mother was English; that he began his career as a geologist—a petrologist; that he holds a degree as a Doctor of Science from the University of London; and that though he is without doubt the most distinguished exponent of the *Philosophia Perennis* in the English-speaking world, he is by no means the advocate of the vague, synthetic "theosophy" vulgarized in our Western world, nor of that theory of "reincarnation"—meaning the return of deceased individuals to rebirth on this earth—which is popularly and erroneously associated in certain circles with Hindu "philosophy." In the hope of clearing the air of such prejudices and misconceptions, I have collected the following biographical details:

Ananda Kentish Coomaraswamy was born on August 22, 1877, in Colombo, Ceylon, the son of a distinguished Ceylonese gentleman, Sir Mutu Coomaraswamy, the first Hindu to have been called to the bar in London, and author of the first translation into English of a Pali Buddhist text. Sir Mutu died before his son was two years old, and the child was brought up in England by his British mother (who survived until 1942).

Ananda Coomaraswamy did not return to his native land until nearly a quarter of a century later. He was educated first at Wycliffe College, at Stonehouse in Gloucestershire, and later at the University of London. Although, without doubt, the Ceylonese youth felt the all-pervading influences of John Ruskin and William Morris, in the awakening nineties, his deeper interests were focused upon science—in particular upon geology and mineralogy. At twenty-two he contributed a paper on "Ceylon Rocks and Graphite" to the *Quarterly Journal of the Geological Society;* and at twenty-five he was appointed director of the Mineralogical Survey of Ceylon. A few years later his work on the geology of Ceylon won him the degree of Doctor of Science from the University of London.

Life in Ceylon opened his eyes to the withering blight cast upon her native arts and crafts by the invasion of Occidental industrialism. Courageously and unequivocally the young Coomaraswamy became the champion of those "native" cultures and handicrafts which were threatened with extermination by the "proselytizing fury" of Occidental civilization.

Since 1917 Coomaraswamy has been with the Boston Museum of Fine Arts, as a research fellow in Oriental art, building up its unsurpassed department of Indian art; collecting, interpreting, expounding to museum curators the traditional philosophy of life and the function of art in human society; demonstrating that all significant expressions, whether in the crafts or in games and other "play," are varying dialects and symbolic activities of one language of the spirit.

Coomaraswamy has been labeled as an expert in Oriental art: but his "Orientalism" has nothing in common with the pseudo-occultism and syncretic theosophistry that are volatilized by the self-appointed prophets of the "cults." He likes to puncture the stereotyped fallacy of the "mysterious" and "mystifying" East, and has asserted that a faithful account of Hinduism might be attained by a categorical denial of most of the statements (e.g. about "reincarnation") that have been made about it not only by European scholars, but even by Indians trained in the contemporary skeptical and evolutionary habits of thinking.

His pen is an instrument of precision. His closely and tightly woven fabric of thought is the very model of explicit denotation —a virtue of written expression that is nowadays being rediscovered. For this scholar the exegesis of ancient texts is above all else a scientific pursuit, considered as means to a more abundant life. He prides himself upon never introducing phrases of his own and never makes any claims for which he cannot cite chapter and verse. His compact, condensed prose often presents a forbidding mosaic on the printed page, offering nothing in the way of enticement to slothful contemporary eyes, but challenging attention nonetheless because of its rigorous exactitude, like that of a mathematical demonstration. Not infrequently matter that would suffice for a whole article is compressed into a footnote. But even when he is thus writing for scholars, it is certainly not only for scholars; and when expressly for those who are not scholars, he can, as the essays in the present collection show, write very simply, relegating footnotes to concluding pages where the reader can ignore them if he so desires.

In the unfolding of this "myriad-minded" intellect—from geology to archaeology and thence to all the arts and expressions, from the humblest to the highest aspirations of all mankind—one is tempted to find a parallel to Leonardo's universal interests.

Beginning, as we have seen, with geology and mineralogy, Coomaraswamy's researches have become universal and all-embracing, ranging from philology in a dozen languages to music and iconography, and from the most ancient metaphysics to the most contemporary problems in politics, sociology, and anthropology. As an admirer has recently stated: "Never has he had time for, nor interest in, presenting personal ideas or novel theories, so constantly and so tirelessly has be devoted his energies to the rediscovery of the truth and the relating of the principles by which cultures rise and fall." Nor does he ever compromise or pull his punches in stating these truths as he has discovered them.

This courage is especially manifest in Coomaraswamy's essays devoted to art. He is today our most eloquent defender of the traditional philosophy of art—the doctrine exemplified in the artifacts that have come down to us from the Middle Ages and the Orient. This philosophy Coomaraswamy has interpreted many times and with a wealth of explicit reference; and in contrast he has pointed out the pathological aspects of our contemporary aesthetes who collect the exotic and the primitive with the greediness of the magpie snatching up bits of colored ribbon with which to "decorate" its nest! The arts of the great timeless tradition move ever from within outward, and are never concerned merely with the idealization of objective fact. Modern art, on the other hand, has no resource or end beyond itself; it is too "fine" to be applied, and too "significant" to mean anything precisely.

For Coomaraswamy, as spokesman of tradition, "disinterested aesthetic contemplation" is a contradiction in terms, and nonsense. The purpose of art has always been, and still should be, effective communication. But what, ask the critics, can works of art communicate? "Let us tell the painful truth," Coomaraswamy retorts, "that most of these works are about God, whom nowadays we never mention in polite society!" One is reminded of the fact that our modern treatises on ukiyoye rarely mention the hetaerae upon whose lives the great part of this art centers. Youthful anthropologists, like Deacon or Tom Harrisson, retracing the continuous-line sand drawings on a lonely beach of the New Hebrides, re-enacting the *dromenon* of the last survivors of a forgotten culture, in this process of feeling-with, may come closer toward understanding alien races, to the heart of true art, than does the most ecstatic and hysterical of Picassolaters in a Fifty-seventh Street gallery. For, to understand and to appreciate the art of any people, one must become united with it in spirit; one must have learned to feel and to understand the cosmos as they have felt and understood it—never approaching them with condescension or contempt, or even with the sort of "objectivity" that, while it may succeed in depicting, always fails to interpret their works and days.

This is not the place to enlarge upon these arresting and challenging ideas. If we are "off the beam" today in our "appreciation of art," as Coomaraswamy diagnoses our current ailment, it may be, as he asserts, because we are living through "one of the two most conspicuous ages of human decadence" —that first being the late classical. Narcissistic exhibitionism and magpie aestheticism—with its greedy acquisition of the irrelevant—are but twin symptoms of our cultural schizophrenia. The manufacture of "art" in studios, coupled with the artless facture of the things that are made in factories, represents for him a reduction of the standard of living to subhuman levels. The coincidence of beauty and utility, significance and aptitude, must determine all human values. Artifacts serving such values are possible only in a co-operative society of free and responsible craftsmen—a vocational society in which men are free to be concerned with the good of the work to be done, and individually responsible for its quality. Coomaraswamy's ideas on art may be studied in *Why Exhibit Works of Art?* and *Figures of Speech or Figures of Thought?* (London: Luzac & Co., 1943, 1946).

Now this traditional philosophy of art is integrated with the whole traditional philosophy of human society, or in other words, and as the readers of the following essays will learn, with the concept of a kingdom of God on earth. Coomaraswamy's work is a monumental achievement in integration: he has become the foremost exponent of the *Philosophia Perennis,* of St. Augustine's "wisdom uncreate, the same now that it ever was, and the same to be forevermore." Across far continents and over centuries and millennia of recorded and unrecorded time, this doctrine speaks in varying dialects, but with a single voice. It is the *sanātana dharma,* the *hagia sophia,* the "justice" or "righteousness" of the tradition, unanimous and universal. All of Coomaraswamy's "myriad-minded" concentra-

tion, together with an almost fabulous self-discipline and pur-
posive "drive," have been yoked together to demonstrate the
single voice of human aspiration. It is we, the contemporaries,
with our genius for fission and division, who are lost—
nous sommes les égarés! "We are at war with ourselves," as
Coomaraswamy insists at the end of his compact essay on René
Guénon, "and *therefore* at war with one another. Western man
is unbalanced, and the question, Can he recover himself? is a
very real one."

Coomaraswamy's essay on Guénon, included in this book,
may be studied as a model of his precision, accuracy, and mathematical brevity. Within the space of a few pages, we are presented with a complete and accurate guide to the intellectual
career of one of the most arresting and most significant of contemporary thinkers. This introduction to Guénon is worth the
price of admission; for the author of *The Reign of Quantity,*
of *East and West,* and *The Crisis of the Modern World* seems
to have been, for the American public at least, one of the
casualties of the war. It is reassuring to know that the *Etudes
Traditionnelles,* the monthly periodical which for many years
had been the vehicle of Guénon's expression, has now resumed
publication. And *Le règne de la quantité* has appeared in book
form in Paris.

I can only hope that the present volume may open the door,
to some readers at least, to a whole "new" realm of thought, as
did my belated discovery of Coomaraswamy some years ago.
Even his footnotes contain more provocative reading and point
the way to more explorations and discoveries than one can ever
find in any of the standard-brand, ready-made, ready-to-wear
opinions proffered in many noisily advertised best sellers.

Robert Allerton Parker.

*New York
March, 1946.*

Chapter I

AM I MY BROTHER'S KEEPER?

CAIN, who killed his brother Abel, the herdsman, and built himself a city, prefigures modern civilization, one that has been described from within as "a murderous machine, with no conscience and no ideals," [1] "neither human nor normal nor Christian," [2] and in fact "an anomaly, not to say a monstrosity." [3] It has been said: "The values of life are slowly ebbing. There remains the show of civilization, without any of its realities." [4] Criticisms such as these could be cited without end. Modern civilization, by its divorce from any principle, can be likened to a headless corpse of which the last motions are convulsive and insignificant. It is not, however, of suicide, but of murder that we propose to speak.

The modern traveler—"thy name is legion"—proposing to visit some "lost paradise" such as Bali, often asks whether or not it has yet been "spoiled." It makes a naïve, and even tragic, confession. For this man does not reflect that he is condemning himself; that what his question asks is whether or not the sources of equilibrium and grace in the other civilizations have yet been poisoned by contact with men like himself and the culture of which he is a product. "The Balinese," as Covarrubias says, "have lived well under a self-sufficient coöperative system, the foundation of which is reciprocal assistance, with money used only as a secondary commodity. Being extremely limited in means to obtain the cash—scarcer every day—to pay taxes and satisfy new needs, it is to be feared that the gradual breaking down of their institutions, together with the drain on their national wealth, will make coolies, thieves, beggars and prostitutes of the proud and honorable Balinese of this generation, and will, in the long run, bring a social and moral catastrophe. . . . It would be futile to recommend measures to prevent the relentless march of Westernization; tourists cannot be kept out, the needs of trade will not be restricted for sentimental [or moral] reasons, and missionary societies are often powerful." [5]

Sir George Watt in 1912 wrote that "however much Indian art may be injured, or individuals suffer, progression in line with the manufacturing enterprise of civilization must be allowed free course." [6] In the same year Gandhi said that "India is being ground down, not under the English heel, but under that of modern civilization." In an open letter to Gilbert Murray, the late Rabindranath Tagore said, "There is no people in the whole of Asia which does not look upon Europe with fear and suspicion." [7] When I said to a working woman that what the Germans were doing in Belgium was very dreadful, she retorted, "Yes, too bad the Belgians should be treated as if they were Congo Negroes."

Modern civilization takes it for granted that people are better off the more things they want and are able to get; its values are quantitative and material. Here, How much is he worth? means How much money has he got? A speaker at Boston College lately described modern Western civilization as a "curse to humanity"; and those who now recognize its reflection in the Japanese mirror are evidently of the same opinion. Nevertheless Henry A. Wallace, then vice-president, in a well-meant speech, promised that when the war should be over, "Older [!] nations will have the privilege to help younger nations get started on the path to industrialization. . . . As their masses learn to read and write, and as they become productive mechanics, their standard of living will double and treble." [8] He did not speak of the price to be paid, or reflect that an incessant "progress," never ending in contentment, means the condemnation of all men to a state of irremediable poverty. In the words of St. Gregory Nazazien,

Could you from all the world all wealth procure,
More would remain, whose lack would leave you poor!

As for reading and writing, we shall only say that the association of these with "productive mechanics" (and the "chain belt" that suggests the "chain gang") is significant, since these arts are only of paramount importance to the masses in a quantitative culture, where one must be able to read both warnings and advertisements if one is to earn money safely and "raise one's standard of living": that if reading and writing are to enable the Indian and Chinese masses to read what the Western proletariat reads, they will remain better off, from any cultural point of view, with their own more classical literature of which all have oral knowledge; and add that it is still true that, as Sir George Birdwood wrote in 1880, "Our education has destroyed their love of their own literature . . . their delight in their own arts and, worst of all, their repose in their own traditional and national religion. It has disgusted them with their own homes—their parents, their sisters, their very wives. It has brought discontent into every family so far as its baneful influences have reached." [9]

Systems of education should be extensions of the cultures of the peoples concerned; but of these the Western educator knows little and cares less. For example, O. L. Reiser assumed that, after the war, American ideals and policies, so far from allowing for other peoples' cultural self-determination, would dominate the world and that all divergent religions and philosophies could and should be discarded in favor of the "scientific humanism" which should now become "the religion of humanity." [10] We can only say that if Western races are in the future to do

anything for the peoples whose cultures have been broken down
in the interests of commerce and "religion," they must begin
by renouncing what has been aptly called their "proselytizing
fury"—"hypocrites, for ye compass sea and land to make one
proselyte." [11]

It is overlooked that while many Asiatic peoples, for reasons
sufficiently obvious, are inadequately provided with the necessities of life, this is by no means true of all Asiatic peoples. In
any case it is overlooked that it is a basic Asiatic conception
that, given the necessaries of life, it is a fallacy to suppose that
the further we can go beyond that the better. Where the European seeks to become economically independent in old age, the
Indian map of life proposes for old age an independence of
economics. The "guinea pigs" of a well-known book, in other
words you and I, whose wants are perpetually exacerbated by
the sight and sound of advertisements (it has been recognized
that "Whole industries are pooling their strength to ram home
a higher standard of living" [12]), have been compared by an
Indian writer [13] to another animal—"the donkey before which
the driver has dangled a much coveted carrot hanging from a
stick fastened to its own harness. The more the animal runs to
get at the carrot, the further is the cart drawn"; i.e. the higher
the dividends paid. We are the donkey, the manufacturer the
driver, and this situation pleases us so well that we, in the kind-
ness of our hearts, would like to make donkeys also of the
Balinese—at the same time that we ask, "Have they been
spoiled yet?" "Spoiled" means "degraded"; but the word has
also another sinister meaning, that of "plundered," and there
are ways of life as well as material goods of which one can be
robbed.

Let us make it clear that if we approach the problem of inter-

cultural relationships largely on the ground of *art*, it is not with
the special modern and aesthetic or sentimental concept of art
in mind, but from that Platonic and once universally human
point of view in which "art" is the principle of manufacture
and nothing but the science of the making of any things whatever for man's good use, physical and metaphysical; and in
which, accordingly, agriculture and cookery, weaving and fish-
ing are just as much arts as painting and music. However
strange this may appear to us, let us remember that we cannot
pretend to think *for* others unless we can think *with* them.
In these contexts, then, "art" involves the whole of the active
life, and presupposes the contemplative. The disintegration of
a people's art is the destruction of their life, by which they are
reduced to the proletarian status of hewers of wood and drawers
of water, in the interests of a foreign trader, whose is the *profit*.
The employment of Malays on rubber estates, for example, in
no way contributes to their culture and certainly cannot have
made them our friends: they owe us nothing. We are irresponsible, in a way that Orientals are not yet, for the most part,
irresponsible.

Let me illustrate what I mean by responsibility. I have
known Indians who indignantly refused to buy shares in a
profitable hotel company, because they would not make money
out of hospitality, and an Indian woman who refused to buy
a washing machine, because then, "What would become of the
washerman's livelihood?" For an equal sense of responsibility
in a European I can cite the infinite pains that Marco Pallis
took, in selecting gifts for his Tibetan friends, not to choose
anything that might tend toward a destruction of the *quality*
of their standard of living.

The modern world has, in fact (as was recently remarked by
Aldous Huxley), abandoned the concept of "right livelihood,"
according to which a man could not be considered a Christian in

good standing if he made his living by usury or speculation, or
considered a Buddhist if he made his living by the manufacture
of weapons or of intoxicating drinks. And as I have said elsewhere, if there are any occupations that are not consistent with
human dignity, or manufactures however profitable that are not
of real *goods*, such occupations and manufactures must be abandoned by any society that has in view the dignity of all its members. It is only when measured in terms of dignity and not
merely in terms of comfort that a "standard of living" can
properly be called "high."

The bases of modern civilization are to such a degree rotten
to the core that it has been forgotten even by the learned that
man ever attempted to live otherwise than by bread alone. It
had been assumed by Plato that "it is contrary to the nature of
the arts to seek the good of anything but their object," [14] and
by St. Thomas Aquinas that "the craftsman is *naturally* inclined by justice to do his work faithfully." [15] To what a level
industrialism must have lowered the workman's sense of honor
and natural will to do a "good job" if, in a reference to the
mechanics and groundmen who make and service airplanes, Gilbert Murray could propound that it is "a quite wonderful
fact that masses of men have been made so trustworthy and
reliable" and could say that "it is the Age of Machines that,
for the first time in history, has made them so." [16] That was a
part of his apology for Western civilization, in an open letter
to Rabindranath Tagore. All that this cock and bull airplane
story really means, of course, is that where production is really
for *use,* and not mainly or only for profit, the workman is *still*
"naturally inclined to do his work faithfully." Even today, as
Mrs. Handy has remarked, "Technical perfection remains the
ideal of the Marquesas Island craftsman." [17] In Europe, the
instinct of workmanship has not been extinguished in human

nature, but only suppressed in human beings working irresponsibly.

Anthropologists, as impartial observers who do not attempt to consider the arts *in vacuo,* but in their relation to the whole structure of society, mince no words in their description of the effects of Western contacts on traditional cultures. Mrs. Handy's record of the Marquesas Islanders, that "the external aspects of their culture have been almost wiped out by the white man's devastating activities," [17] is typical of what could be cited from a hundred other sources. Of the "savages" of New Guinea Raymond Firth says that "their art as an expression of complex social values is of basic importance," but that under European influence "in nearly every case the quality of their art has begun to fall off." [18] C. F. Iklé writes that due to the influence of the Western world "which is so ready to flood the remainder of our globe with inferior mass products, thus destroying among native peoples the concepts of quality and beauty, together with the joy of creation . . . it is a question whether the beautiful art of Ikàt weaving can long survive in the Dutch East Indies." [19]

It is true that we have learned to appreciate the "primitive arts"; but only when we have "collected" them. We "preserve" folk songs, at the same time that our way of life destroys the singer. We are proud of our museums, where we display the damning evidence of a way of living that we have made impossible. These museum "treasures" were originally the everyday productions of live men; but now, "due to the breakdown of culture in the islands where the objects were made, they may be studied more satisfactorily in museums," while at their source these "highly developed and beautiful techniques have died, or are dying." [20] "Dying," because in the words of the knighted fatalist, "progression in line with the manufacturing enterprise of modern civilization must be allowed free course"! To which we can only rejoin that, if it *must* be that offenses come, "Woe unto them through whom they come." What, indeed, has lately happened to the cities that Cain built? Let us not assume that "it can't happen here."

Our "love of art" and "appreciation" of primitive art, as we call whatever art is abstract and impersonal, rather than self-expressive or exhibitionist, has not aroused in our hearts any love for the primitive artist himself. A more loveless, and at the same time more sentimentally cynical, culture than that of modern Europe and America it would be impossible to imagine. "Seeing through," as it supposes, everything, it cares for nothing but itself. The passionless reason of its "objective" scholarship, applied to the study of "what men have believed," is only a sort of frivolity, in which the real problem, that of knowing what should be believed, is evaded. Values are to such an extent inverted that action, properly means to an end, has been made an end in itself, and contemplation, prerequisite to action, has come to be disparaged as an "escape" from the responsibilties of activity.

In the present essay we are concerned, not with the political or economic, but with the cultural relations that have actually subsisted, and on the other hand should subsist, as between the peoples who call themselves progressive and those whom they call backward, a type of nomenclature that belongs to the genus of "the lion painted by himself." Not that we overlook the sinister relationships that connect your cultural activities abroad with your political and economic interests, but that there is the imminent danger that even when you have made up your minds to establish political and economic relations with others on a basis of justice, you will still believe that you have been entrusted with a "civilizing mission." There is more than political and economic interest behind the proselytizing fury;

behind all this there is a fanaticism that cannot away with any sort of wisdom that is not of its own date and kind and the product of its own pragmatic calculations; "there is a rancor," as Hermes Trismegistus said, "that is contemptuous of immortality, and will not let us recognize what is divine in us." [21]

That is why the export of your "education" is even more nefarious than your traffic in arms. What was attempted by the English in India when they proposed to build up a class of persons "Indian in blood and color, but English in tastes, in opinion, in morals and in intellect" (Lord Macaulay) is just what Middletown, substituting "American" for "English," would like to do today. It is what the British tried to do in Ireland where "in thirty years Irish was killed off so rapidly that the whole island contained fewer speakers in 1891 than the small province of Connaught alone did thirty years before. . . . The amount of horrible suffering entailed by this policy . . . counted for nothing with the Board of National Education, compared with their great object of . . . the attainment of one Anglified uniformity. . . . The children are taught, if nothing else, to be ashamed of their own parents, ashamed of their own nationality, ashamed of their own names." [22] Everyone will recognize the pattern, repeated alike in the case of the "English-educated" Indian and in that of the American Indian who has been subjected to the untaught ignorance of public school teachers who cannot speak his mother tongue.

Such are the fruits of "civilization," and the fruit betrays the tree. All that can only be atoned for by repentance, recantation, and restitution. Of these, the last is a virtual impossibility; the fallen redwood cannot be replanted. A traditional culture still, however, survives precariously in "unspoiled" oases, and the least that we can say to the modern world is this: Whatever else you dispense in "wars of pacification" or by way of "peaceful penetration," be good enough to reserve your "college education" and your "finishing schools" for home consumption. What you call your "civilizing mission" is in our eyes nothing but a form of megalomania. Whatever we need to learn from you, we shall come to ask you for as the need is felt. At the same time, if you choose to visit us, you will be welcome guests, and if there is anything of ours that you admire, we shall say, "It is yours."

For the rest, it is much more for its own sake than in order to make restitution that the modern world must "change its mind" (repent); for, as Philosophia said to Boethius in his distress, "You have forgotten who you are." But how can this "reasoning and mortal animal," this extroverted mentality, be awakened, reminded of itself, and converted from its sentimentality and its sole reliance on estimative knowledge to the life of the intellect? How can this world be given back its meaning? Not, of course, by a return to the outward forms of the Middle Ages nor, on the other hand, by assimilation to any surviving, Oriental or other, pattern of life. But why not by a recognition of the principles on which the patterns were based? These principles, on which the "unspoiled" life of the East is still supported, must at least be grasped, respected, and understood if ever the Western provincial is to become a citizen of the world. Even the goodness of the modern world is unprincipled; its "altruism" is no longer founded on a knowledge of the Self of all beings and therefore in the love of Self, but only on selfish inclination. And what of those who are not inclined to be unselfish; is there any intellectual standard by which they can be blamed?

If ever the gulf between East and West, of which we are made continually more aware as physical intimacies are forced upon us, is to be bridged, it will be only by an agreement on principles, and not by any participation in common forms of government or methods of manufacture and distribution. It is not, as Kierkegaard said, new forms of government, but another Socrates that the world needs. A philosophy identical with Plato's is still a living force in the East. We called the modern world a headless body; in the Eastern books there is a teaching, how to put heads on bodies again. It is one of sacrifice and of preoccupation with realities; outwardly a rite and inwardly a being born again.

To propose an agreement on principles does not involve or imply that the Western world should be Orientalized; propaganda is out of the question as between gentlemen, and everyone must make use of the forms appropriate to his own psychophysical constitution. It is the European that wants to practice Yoga; the Oriental points out that he has already contemplative disciplines of his own. What is implied is that a recognition of the principles by which the East still lives, and which can, therefore, be seen in operation (and few will question that peoples as yet "unspoiled" are happier than those that have been "spoiled"), could lead the modern "world of impoverished reality," in which it is maintained that "such knowledge as is not empirical is meaningless," back to the philosopher who denied the dependence of knowledge on sensation and maintained that all learning is recollection.

They cannot help us who, in the words of Plato, "think that nothing is, except what they can grasp firmly with their hands." I repeat what I have said elsewhere, that "the European, for his own sake and all men's sake in a future world, must not only cease to harm and exploit the other peoples of the world, but must also give up the cherished and flattering belief that he can do them any good otherwise than by being good himself." I am far from believing that the European is incapable of goodness.

In conclusion, let me say that the few European workers in the Eastern field to whom my criticisms do not apply will be the last to disagree with them. Also, that what I have been saying is not what you will hear from the already English-educated and too often "spoiled" Orientals with whom you are able to converse.[23] I am speaking for a majority, literate and illiterate, that is not vocal, partly by inclination, and partly because, in more than one sense, they do not speak your language. I am speaking for those who once before "bowed low before the West in patient, deep disdain," and are not less a power today because you cannot know or hear them.

REFERENCES

[1] G. La Piana, in *Harvard Divinity School Bulletin*, XXVII, p. 27.
[2] Eric Gill, *Autobiography* (New York, 1942), p. 174.
[3] René Guénon, *East and West* (London, 1941), p. 43.
[4] A. N. Whitehead, *Adventures of Ideas* (1933), p. 358.
[5] M. Covarrubias, *Island of Bali* (1942). Cf. Colin McPhee, "Ankloeng Gamelans in Bali," *Djawa*, Nos. 5 and 6, 17de Jaargang (September-December, 1937), p. 348: "The last five years, what with the changing tempo of life, the benefits of education, have seen the most rapid changes of all, the most irresponsible patching together of heterogeneous elements in music and drama. One wonders what will survive in ten years of what was once an art." Before we can talk wisely about co-operation it must first of all be realized that, as the editor of the *New English Weekly* recently remarked, "practically the whole of Oriental humanity, the greater portion of the human race, including the U.S.S.R., lives in a social aspiration which is the polar opposite of the American." Any possibilities of co-operation are bound up with agreement about ends, whereas almost every proposal nowadays brought forward has only to do with means, and usually with the application of Western means to Eastern situations.
[6] Sir George Watt, *Indian Art at Delhi* (London, 1912), p. 72. This is the modern form of the Amaurian (Amalrician) heresy; the economically determined man, without free will, is by the same token irresponsible; no blame to him, the fault is fate's! Cf. Sir George Birdwood, *Sva*, pp. 84-5: "England . . . where every national

interest is sacrificed to the shibboleth of unrestricted international competition; and where as a consequence, agriculture, the only sure foundation of society, languishes . . . its last result, the bitter, stark and cruel contrast presented between the West End of London and the East. And do Europe and America desire to reduce all Asia to an East End?" And K. E. Barlow (in *Purpose,* XI, 1939, p. 245): "In our everyday world the principle of exploitation without responsibility has brought a disorder in society and in Nature which stupefies all of us who think. . . . It has become clear that our civilisation is pursuing a course which cannot long be maintained."

[7] Rabindranath Tagore and Gilbert Murray, *Open Letters, East and West* (Paris, 1932), p. 44.

[8] Henry A. Wallace, then vice-president, in a speech, 1943. And as the late President Roosevelt truly said, "Never again must we in the United States isolate ourselves from the rest of humanity"; but he showed by his next words, "I am confident that the foreign trade of the United States can be trebled after the war—providing millions more jobs," that he had not in mind the root of the matter, that is, an abandonment of America's *cultural* isolation. As for the "price" of industrialism, it must be recognized, in the first place, that the American "standard of living," judged by qualitative standards, is beneath contempt, at the same time that the artist, no longer a member of society but a parasite upon it, "has become the pekinese of the rich" (Erich Meissner's phrase in *Germany in Peril,* 1942, p. 42). "The standardised products of our mills and factories are a disgrace to American civilisation" (Msgr. G. B. O'Toole in Foreword to Krzesinski, *Is Modern Culture Doomed?* 1942). On the salesman's and producer's side: "Modern machinery and its irresistible advance fills these men with mystic frenzy" (Meissner, *ibid.,* p. 115): and, "Eventually Man . . . adopts a discipline which transforms him into a machine himself" (Ernst Niekisch, quoted by Meissner, *ibid.*). Vice-President Wallace's words and two current, and very revealing, American advertisements are a dramatic demonstration. Of the advertisements, one, depicting a salesman behind his counter, puts into his mouth the words: "Handmade? Of course not! Why, most everything in this store is made by machines nowadays. If it weren't I wouldn't be selling half these things, and you couldn't buy them. They'd cost too much." The other prints a "poem," called "My Machine," and its first lines are:

> There are many other machines, but this one is mine.
> It is a part of me, I am a part of it.
> *We are one.*
> *It does not stop*—unless I forget.

There is no reference to the quality, either of man or of product, in either case.

"On peut remarquer que la machine est, en un certain sens, le contraire de l'outil, et non point un 'outil perfectionné' comme beaucoup se l'imaginent, car l'outil est en quelque sort un 'prolongement' de l'homme lui-même, tandis que la machine réduit celui-çi à n'être plus que son serviteur ["minder"]; et, si l'on a pu dire que 'l'outil engendra le métier,' il n'est pas moins vrai que la machine le tue; les réactions instinctives des artisans contre les premières machines s'expliquent par là d'elle-mêmes" (René Guénon, *Le règne de la quantité et les signes des temps*, 2nd ed.; Paris, 1945, p. 64, note). In Ruskin's words, "The great cry that rises from all our manufacturing cities, louder than their furnace blast, is all in very deed for this,—that we manufacture everything there except men" (*Stones of Venice*, in Ruskin's works, Vol. X, p. 196): and, "This evil cannot be cured through higher wages, good housing conditions and improved nutrition" (Meissner, *ibid.*, p. 42). "If your real ideals are those of materialistic efficiency, then the sooner you know your own mind, and face the consequences, the better. . . . The more highly industrialised a country, the more easily a materialistic philosophy will flourish in it, and the more deadly that philosophy will be. . . . And the tendency of unlimited industrialism is to create masses of men and women—detached from tradition, alienated from religion, and susceptible to mass suggestion: in other words, a mob. And a mob will be no less a mob if it is well fed, well clothed, well housed, and well disciplined" (T. S. Eliot in *The Idea of a Christian Society*).

"It is doubtful whether life can be significantly lived without conscious relation to some tradition. Those who do live without it live as a kind of moral proletariat, without roots and without loyalties. For to be significant life needs form, and form is the outcome of a quality of thought and feeling which shapes a tradition" (Dorothy M. Emmet in *The Nature of Metaphysical Thinking*, 1946, p. 163).

More than a physical well-being is necessary for felicity. An Indian peasant's face has neither the vacancy of the grinning apes and whores that are the ideal of the American advertiser, nor the expression of anxiety that marks the American "common man" in real life. "In spite of our enormous technological advances we are spiritually, and as humane beings, not the equals of the average Australian aboriginal or the average Eskimo—we are very definitely their inferiors" (M. F. Ashley Montagu, "Socio-Biology of Man," *Scientific Monthly,* June, 1942, p. 49).

[9] Sir John Birdwood, *Industrial Arts of India* (1880).

[10] O. L. Reiser, *A New Earth and a New Humanity* (New York, 1942), p. 209.

[11] Matthew 23:15.

[12] "It is open to question whether anything a machine turns out for direct human use is productive of human good" (in the *Nation,* November 27, 1943). Cf. L. Ziegler in *Forum Philosophicum* I, 87, 88: "Every ware which does not answer an existing need is above all the most superfluous thing in the world . . . it must first artificially rouse up a need in places where a need does not exist. . . . Present day economic management is framed for the stimulation, yes, even for the 'creation' of needs . . . as if wages and income could in any way keep pace with this artificially aroused need for a commodity. . . . The fashionably altering display of goods attaches to so unlimited a mass and variety of wares a label of necessity, that in the face of it even the purchasing power of the rich is beaten, whereas the poor seem doomed to a poverty hitherto undreamt of. From this point of view modern finance reveals itself as the enemy of society, yes, even as the destroyer of society." For, observe that, as Albert Schweitzer says, "Whenever the timber trade is good, permanent famine reigns in the Ogowe region." Modern wars, in fact, are fought for world markets; in other words, in order that all "backward" peoples may be forced to purchase an annual quota of gadgets from those who call themselves "advanced."

Here it is, however, with the moral effects of manufacture for profit that we are concerned, and especially with its effect on those who are forced on the one hand to provide the raw materials, and on the other to buy the manufactured gadgets. It is not merely that the change from a barter to a money economy is actually "from an economy of abundance to one of scarcity" (Parsons, *Pueblo Indian Religion,* 1939, p. 1144), but that it is a matter of the poisoning of the lives of contented peoples, whose culture is destroyed to satisfy the saurian greed of the plutocratic "democracies." In the Balkans, for example, "There were two sorts of people. There was the people as it had been since the beginning of time, working in the villages, small towns and capitals. But there was also a new people, begotten by the new towns which the industrial and financial development of the nineteenth century had raised all over Europe. . . . This new sort of people [was one that] had been defrauded of their racial tradition, they enjoyed no inheritance of wisdom; brought up without gardens, to work on machines, all but a few lacked the education which is given by craftsmanship; and they needed this wisdom and this education as never before, because they were living in conditions of unprecedented frustration and insecurity" (Rebecca West, in *Black Lamb and Grey Falcon*).

"The rise of science, the discrediting of religion, and the abiding triumph of capitalism have focussed the basic personality of Western man upon one goal, success, the only proof of which is the endless acquisition of money. . . . But this kind of training, as it emphasizes striving for self-esteem and success, releases at the same time the extraordinary aggressiveness which takes so many cruel forms. Aggressiveness turned inward results in masochism, feelings of inferiority, passivity, and other kinds of weakness. Turned outward, the result is sadism, extreme rivalry, envy, and conflict, the social climax being war. Competition, which motivates the entire psychological formation, is not in itself evil, since it may create a strong and self-reliant human being; but in a scarcity economy such as ours the combination of the social system with a basic personality focussed on competition for success overburdens the lives of most human beings with tensions and insecurities for which only one term is adequate—lifelong neuroticism" (Delmore Schwartz, reviewing Abram Kardiner, *The Individual and His Society* and *The Psychological Frontiers of Society*, 1939 and 1945, in *The Nation*, Jan. 12, 1946, pp. 46-48).

There can be no possible doubt that what men now understand by "civilization" is an essentially vicious and destructive force, or that what is called "progress" is both suicidal and murderous. "Civilisation, as we now have it, can only end in disaster" (G. H. Estabrooks, *Man the Mechanical Misfit*, New York, 1941, p. 246); or as C. H. Grattan and G. R. Leighton so well say, "No one looking for peace and quiet has any business talking about international trade" (in

Harper's Magazine, August, 1944). Of all these things the catastrophes of today are only a beginning.

[13] J. C. Kumarappa. Cf. Philo Judaeus, *De specialibus legibus* IV, 80 f.

[14] *Republic,* 342 B, 347 A, etc.

[15] *Summa Theologica,* I-II, 57, 3 and 2. *Justitia* here = δικαιοσύνη = *dharma,* here as in Plato, *Republic,* 433 A, and in Matthew 6:33, where the word is rendered by "righteousness," with some loss of force.

[16] *Open Letters, East and West.*

[17] *Art des Îles Marquises* (1938). Cf. the words of two reviewers of J. F. Embree's *Suye Mura, a Japanese Village:* One remarks that here "we see a little group of Japanese families living, working, struggling in their daily life to earn their bread, to educate their children, and to live out lives of ordinary usefulness, in the way common to people everywhere"; the other that "his book offers good evidence that it will take many a long year to Westernize the Japanese peasant." The more "long years" the better for the peace and happiness of the Japanese peasants and of the world!

Contrast also the words of H. N. Brailsford, "The caste line will have to be broken, if industrial work is to be provided for the superfluous cultivators," with those of the sociologist S. Chandrasekhar, who points out that "the development of cotton textile-mill industry in India, which today employs about 430,000 workers, has actually been responsible for throwing out of employment an estimated total of 6 million handloom workers, who have been forced to fall back upon an already overcrowded agrarian economy"; and consider whether Gandhi's cult of the spinning wheel is not a more practical and realistic way of dealing with India's poverty than Mr. Brailsford's.

[18] *Art and Life in New Guinea* (1936), pp. 31, 32. Cf. Tom Harrisson, *Savage Civilisation, passim.*

[19] *Bobbin and Needle Club* (New York, 1931), XV, p. 56.

[20] G. A. Reichard, *Melanesian Design* (1931), pp. 1, 90.

A Ceylonese correspondent recently asked me: "If God appeared on earth, and inquired for the Aztecs, Incas, Red Indians, Australian aborigines, and other slowly disappearing races, would the civilized nations take him to your great museum?"

[21] Asclepius 1.12 b (Scott, *Hermetica,* I.309).

[22] Douglas Hyde, *Literary History of Ireland* (1899), pp. 630-44.

²³ For example, Professor F. S. C. Northrop in his *Meeting of East and West*, 1946, p. 434, quotes the "cultivated humanist" Jawaharlal Nehru to prove that "the younger Indians and other Orientals" are anxious to learn "what the West has to teach of science and its applications," which is true enough, but hardly to the point in a book intended to show that Eastern and Western ideologies are unlike; he overlooks Shri Bharata Kumarappa, who says that "we must be clear in our minds as to what exactly we want to work for—mere material prosperity or human development," and complains that among socialists "the question of whether an abundance of goods is necessary for human well-being is never so much as raised."

Chapter II

THE BUGBEAR OF LITERACY

IT WAS possible for Aristotle,[1] starting from the premise that a man, being actually cultured, may *also* become literate, to ask whether there is a necessary or merely an accidental connection of literacy with culture. Such a question can hardly arise for us, to whom illiteracy implies, as a matter of course, ignorance, backwardness, unfitness for self-government: for us, unlettered peoples are uncivilized peoples, and vice versa—as a recent publisher's blurb expresses it: "The greatest force in civilization is the collective wisdom of a literate people."

There are reasons for this point of view; they inhere in the distinction of a people, or folk, from a proletariat, that of a social organism from a human ant heap. For a proletariat, literacy is a practical and cultural necessity. We may remark in passing that necessities are not always goods in themselves, out of their context; some, like wooden legs, are advantageous only to men already maimed. However that may be, it remains that literacy is a necessity *for us,* and from both points of view; (1) because our industrial system can only be operated and profits can only be made by men provided with at least an elementary knowledge of the "three R's"; and (2) because, where there is no longer any necessary connection between one's "skill" (now a timesaving "economy of motion" rather than a control of the product) and one's "wisdom," the possibility of culture depends so much on our ability to read the best books. We say "possibility" here because, whereas the literacy actually produced by compulsory mass education often involves little or no more than an ability and the will to read the newspapers and advertisements, an actually cultured man under these conditions will be one who has studied many books in many languages, and this is not a kind of knowledge that can be handed out to everyone under "compulsion" (even if *any* nation could afford the needed quantity and quality of teachers) or that could be acquired by everyone, however ambitious.

We have allowed that in industrial societies, where it is assumed that man is made for commerce and where men are cultured, if at all, in spite of rather than because of their environment, literacy is a necessary skill. It will naturally follow that *if*, on the principle that misery loves company, we are planning to industrialize the rest of the world, we are also in duty bound to train it in Basic English, or words to that effect —American is already a language of exclusively external relationships, a tradesman's tongue—lest the other peoples should be unable to compete effectively with us. Competition is the life of trade, and gangsters must have rivals.

In the present article we are concerned with something else, viz., the assumption that, even for societies not yet industrialized, literacy is "an unqualified good and an indispensible condition of culture." [2] The vast majority of the world's population is still unindustrialized and unlettered, and there are peoples still "unspoiled" (in the interior of Borneo): but the average American who knows of no other way of living than his own, judges that "unlettered" means "uncultured," *as if* this majority consisted only of a depressed class in the context of his own environment. It is because of this, as well as for some meaner reasons, not unrelated to "imperial" interests, that when we propose not merely to exploit but also to educate "the lesser breeds without the [i.e. *our*] law" we inflict upon them profound, and often lethal, injuries. We say "lethal" rather than "fatal" here because it is precisely a destruction of their *memories* that is involved. We overlook that "education" is never

creative, but a two-edged weapon, always destructive; whether
of ignorance or of knowledge depending upon the educator's
wisdom or folly. Too often fools rush in where angels might
fear to tread.

As against the complacent prejudice we shall essay to show
(1) that there is no necessary connection of literacy with culture, and (2) that to impose our literacy (and our contemporary "literature") upon a cultured but illiterate people is to
destroy their culture in the name of our own. For the sake of
brevity we shall assume without argument that "culture" implies an ideal quality and a good form that can be realized by
all men irrespective of condition: and, since we are treating of
culture chiefly as expressed in words, we shall identify culture
with "poetry"; not having in view the kind of poetry that
nowadays babbles of green fields or that merely reflects social
behavior or our private reactions to passing events, but with
reference to that whole class of prophetic literature that includes
the Bible, the Vedas, the Edda, the great epics, and in general
the world's "best books," and the most philosophical if we
agree with Plato that "wonder is the beginning of philosophy."
Of these "books" many existed long before they were written
down, many have never been written down, and others have
been or will be lost.

We shall have now to make some quotations from the works
of men whose "culture" cannot be called in question; for while
the merely literate are often very proud of their literacy, such
as it is, it is only by men who are "not only literate but also
cultured" that it has been widely recognized that "letters" at
their best are only a means to an end and never an end in themselves, or, indeed, that "the letter kills." A "literary" man, if
ever there was one, the late Professor G. L. Kittredge writes: [3]
"It requires a combined effort of the reason and the imagination
to conceive a poet as a person who cannot write, singing or re-

citing his verses to an audience that cannot read. . . . The ability of oral tradition to transmit great masses of verse for hundreds of years is proved and admitted. . . . To this oral literature, as the French call it, education is no friend. Culture destroys it, sometimes with amazing rapidity. *When a nation begins to read . . . what was once the possession of the folk as a whole, becomes the heritage of the illiterate only, and soon, unless it is gathered up by the antiquary, vanishes altogether.*" Mark, too, that this oral literature once belonged "to the whole people . . . the community whose intellectual interests are the same from the top of the social structure to the bottom," while in the reading society it is accessible only to antiquaries, and is no longer bound up with everyday life. A point of further importance is this: that the traditional oral literatures interested not only all *classes,* but also all *ages* of the population; while the books that are nowadays written expressly "for children" are such as no mature mind could tolerate; it is now only the comic strips that appeal alike to children who have been given nothing better and at the same time to "adults" who have never grown up.

It is in just the same way that music is thrown away; folk songs are lost to the people at the same time that they are collected and "put in a bag"; and in the same way that the "preservation" of a people's art in folk museums is a funeral rite, for preservatives are only necessary when the patient has already died. Nor must we suppose that "community singing" can take the place of folk song; its level can be no higher than that of the Basic English in which our undergraduates must be similarly drilled, if they are to understand even the language of their elementary textbooks.

In other words, "Universal compulsory education, of the type introduced at the end of the last century, has not fulfilled expectations by producing happier and more effective citizens; on

THE BUGBEAR OF LITERACY

the contrary, it has created readers of the yellow press and cinema-goers" (Karl Otten). A master who can himself not only read, but also *write* good classical Latin and Greek, remarks that "there is no doubt of the quantitative increase in literacy of a kind, and amid the general satisfaction that something is being multiplied it escapes enquiry whether the something is profit or deficit." He is discussing only the "worst effects" of enforced literacy, and concludes: "Learning and wisdom have often been divided; perhaps the clearest result of modern literacy has been to maintain and enlarge the gulf." [2]

Douglas Hyde remarks that "in vain have disinterested visitors opened wide eyes of astonishment at schoolmasters who knew no Irish being appointed to teach pupils who knew no English. . . . Intelligent children endowed with a vocabulary in every day use of about three thousand words enter the Schools of the Chief Commissioner, to come out at the end with their natural vivacity gone, their intelligence almost completely sapped, their splendid command of their native language lost forever, and a vocabulary of five or six hundred English words, badly pronounced and barbarously employed, substituted for it. . . . Story, lay, poem, song, aphorism, proverb, and the unique stock in trade of an Irish speaker's mind, is gone forever, *and replaced by nothing.* . . . The children are taught, if nothing else, to be ashamed of their own parents, ashamed of their own nationality, ashamed of their own names. . . . It is a remarkable system of 'education' " [4]—this system that you, "civilized and literate" Americans, have inflicted upon your own Amerindians, and that all imperial races are still inflicting upon their subjected peoples, and would like to impose upon their allies—the Chinese, for example.

The problem involved is both of languages and what is said in them. As for language, let us bear in mind, in the first place, that no such thing as a "primitive language," in the sense of one having a limited vocabulary fitted only to express the simplest external relationships, is known. Much rather, that is a condition to which, under certain circumstances and as the result of "nothing-morist" philosophies, languages tend, rather than one from which they originate; for example, 90 per cent of our American "literacy" is a two-syllabled affair.[5]

In the seventeenth century Robert Knox said of the Sinhalese that "their ordinary Plow-men and Husbandmen do speak elegantly, and are full of complement. And there is no difference of ability and speech of a Country-man and a Courtier."[6] Abundant testimony to the like effect could be cited from all over the world. Thus of Gaelic, J. F. Campbell wrote, "I am inclined to think that dialect the best which is spoken by the most illiterate in the islands . . . men with clear heads and wonderful memories, generally very poor and old, living in remote corners of remote islands, and speaking only Gaelic,"[7] and he quotes Hector Maclean, who says that the loss of their oral literature is due "partly to reading . . . partly to bigoted religious ideas, and partly to narrow utilitarian views"—which are, precisely, the three typical forms in which modern civilization impresses itself upon the older cultures. Alexander Carmichael says that "the people of Lews, like the people of the Highlands and Islands generally, carry the Scriptures in their minds and apply them in their speech. . . . Perhaps no people had a fuller ritual of song and story, of secular rite and religious ceremony . . . than the ill-understood and so-called illiterate Highlanders of Scotland."[8]

St. Barbe Baker tells us that in Central Africa "my trusted friend and companion was an old man who could not read or write, though well versed in stories of the past. . . . The old chiefs listened enthralled. . . . Under the present system of education there is grave risk that much of this may be lost."[9] W. G. Archer points out that "unlike the English system in which one could pass one's life without coming into contact with poetry, the Uraon tribal system uses poetry as a vital appendix to dancing, marriages and the cultivation of a crop—functions in which all Uraons join as a part of their tribal life," adding that "if we have to single out the factor which caused the decline of English village culture, we should have to say it was literacy." [10] In an older England, as Prior and Gardner remind us, "even the ignorant and unlettered man could read the meaning of sculptures that now only trained archeologists can interpret." [11]

The anthropologist Paul Radin points out that "the distortion in our whole psychic life and in our whole apperception of the external realities produced by the invention of the alphabet, the whole tendency of which has been to elevate thought and thinking to the rank of the exclusive proof of all verities, never occurred among primitive peoples," adding that "it must be explicitly recognized that in temperament and in capacity for logical and symbolical thought, there is no difference between civilized and primitive man," and as to "progress," that none in ethnology will ever be achieved "until scholars rid themselves, once and for all, of the curious notion that everything possesses an evolutionary history; until they realize that certain ideas and certain concepts are as ultimate for man" [12] as his physical constitution. "The distinction of peoples in a state of nature from civilized peoples can no longer be maintained." [13]

We have so far considered only the dicta of literary men. A really "savage" situation and point of view are recorded by Tom Harrisson, from the New Hebrides. "The children are educated by listening and watching. . . . Without writing, memory is perfect, tradition exact. The growing child is taught all that is known. . . . Intangible things cooperate in every effort of making, from conception to canoe-building. . . . Songs are a form of story-telling. . . . The lay-out and content in the thousand myths which every child learns (often word perfect, and one story may last for hours) are a whole library . . . the hearers are held in a web of spun words"; they converse together "with that accuracy and pattern of beauty in words that we have lost." And what do they think of us? "The natives easily learn to write after white impact. They regard it as a curious and useless performance. They say: 'Cannot a man remember and speak?' " [14] They consider us "mad," and may be right.

When we set out to "educate" the South Sea Islanders it is generally in order to make them more useful to ourselves (this was admittedly the beginning of "English education" in India), or to "convert" them to our way of thinking; not having in view to introduce them to Plato. But if we or they should happen upon Plato, it might startle both to find that their protest, "Cannot a man *remember?*" is also his.[15] "For," he says, "this invention [of letters] will produce forgetfulness in the minds of those who learn to use it, because they will not exercise their memory. Their trust in writing, produced by external characters which are no part of themselves, will discourage the use of their own memory within them. You have invented an elixir *not of memory, but of reminding;* and you offer your pupils the appearance of wisdom, not true wisdom, for they will read many things without teaching, and will therefore seem to know many things [Professor E. K. Rand's "more and more of less and less"], when they are for the most part ignorant and hard to get along with, since they are not wise but only wiseacres." He goes on to say that there is another kind of "word," of higher origin and greater power than the written (or as we should say, the printed) word; and maintains that the wise man, *"when in earnest,* will not write in ink" dead words that cannot teach the truth effectively, but will sow the seeds of wisdom in souls that are able to receive them and so "to pass them on forever."

There is nothing strange or peculiar in Plato's point of view;

THE BUGBEAR OF LITERACY

it is one, for example, with which every cultured Indian un-
affected by modern European influences would agree wholly. It
will suffice to cite that great scholar of Indian languages, Sir
George A. Grierson, who says that "the ancient Indian system
by which literature is recorded not on paper but on the memory,
and carried down from generation to generation of teachers and
pupils, is still [1920] in complete survival in Kashmir. Such
fleshly tables of the heart are often more trustworthy than birch
bark or paper manuscripts. The reciters, even when learned
Pandits, take every care to deliver the messages word for word,"
and records taken down from professional storytellers are thus
"in some respects more valuable than any written manu-
script." [16]

From the Indian point of view a man can only be said to
know what he knows *by heart;* what he must go to a book to
be reminded of, he merely knows of. There are hundreds of
thousands of Indians even now who daily repeat from knowledge by heart either the whole or some large part of the *Bhagavad Gītā;* others more learned can recite hundreds of thousands
of verses of longer texts. It was from a traveling village singer in
Kashmir that I first heard sung the Odes of the classical Persian
poet, Jalālu'd-Dīn Rūmī. From the earliest times, Indians have
thought of the learned man, not as one who has read much, but
as one who has been profoundly taught. It is much rather from
a master than from any book that wisdom can be learned.

We come now to the last part of our problem, which has to
do with the characteristic preoccupations of the oral and the
written literature; for although no hard and fast line can be
drawn between them, there is a qualitative and thematic distinction, as between literatures that were originally oral and
those that are created, so to speak, on paper—"In the beginning
was the WORD." The distinction is largely of poetry from
prose and myth from fact. The quality of oral literature is essen-

tially poetical, its content essentially mythical, and its preoccupation with the spiritual adventures of heroes: the quality of originally written literature is essentially prosaic, its content literal, and its preoccupation with secular events and with personalities. In saying "poetical" we mean to imply "mantic," and are naturally taking for granted that the "poetic" is a literary *quality,* and not merely a literary (versified) form. Contemporary poetry is essentially and inevitably of the same caliber as modern prose; both are equally opinionated, and the best in either embodies a few "happy thoughts" rather than any certainty. As a famous gloss expresses it, "Unbelief is for the mob." We who can call an art "significant," knowing not of what, are also proud to "progress," we know not whither.

Plato maintains that one who is *in earnest* will not write, but teach; and that if the wise man writes at all, it will be either only for amusement—mere "belles lettres"—or to provide reminders for himself when his memory is weakened by old age. We know exactly what Plato means by the words "in earnest"; it is not about human affairs or personalities, but about the eternal verities, the nature of real being, and the nourishment of our immortal part, that the wise man will be in earnest. Our mortal part can survive "by bread alone," but it is by the Myth that our Inner Man is fed; or, if we substitute for the true myths the propagandist myths of "race," "uplift," "progress," and "civilizing mission," the Inner Man starves. The written text, as Plato says, *can* serve those whose memories have been weakened by old age. Thus it is that in the senility of culture we have found it necessary to "preserve" the masterpieces of art in museums, and at the same time to record in writing and so also to "preserve" (if only for scholars) as much as can be "collected" of oral literatures that would otherwise be lost forever; and this must be done before it is *too late.*

All serious students of human societies are agreed that agriculture and handicraft are essential foundations of any civilization; the primary meaning of the word being that of making a *home* for oneself. But, as Albert Schweitzer says, "We proceed as if not agriculture and handicraft, but reading and writing were the beginning of civilization," and, "from schools which are mere copies of those of Europe they ["natives"] are turned out as 'educated' persons, that is, who think themselves superior to manual work, and want to follow only commercial or intellectual callings . . . those who go through the schools are mostly lost to agriculture and handicraft." [17] As that great missionary, Charles Johnson of Zululand, also said, "the central idea [of the mission schools] was to prize individuals off the mass of the national life."

Our literary figures of thought, for example, the notions of "culture" (analogous to agriculture), "wisdom" (originally "skill"), and "asceticism" (originally "hard work"), are derived from the productive and constructive arts; for, as St. Bonaventura says, "There is nothing therein which does not bespeak a true wisdom, and it is for this reason that Holy Scripture very properly makes use of such similes." [18] In normal societies, the necessary labors of production and construction are no mere "jobs," but also rites, and the poetry and music that are associated with them are a kind of liturgy. The "lesser mysteries" of the crafts are a natural preparation for the greater "mysteries of the kingdom of heaven." But for us, who can no longer think in terms of Plato's divine "justice" of which the social aspect is vocational, that Christ was a carpenter and the son of a carpenter was only an historical accident; we read, but do not understand that where we speak of primary matter as "wood," we must also speak of Him "through whom all things were made" as a "carpenter." At the best, we interpret the classical figures of thought, not in their universality but as figures of speech invented by individual authors. Where literacy

becomes an only skill, "the collective wisdom of a literate
people" may be only a collective ignorance—while "backward communities are the oral libraries of the world's ancient
cultures." [19]

The purpose of our educational activities abroad is to assimi-
late our pupils to our ways of thinking and living. It is not easy
for any foreign teacher to acknowledge Ruskin's truth, that
there is one way only to help others, and that that is, not to
train them in our way of living (however bigoted our faith in
it may be), but to find out what they have been trying to do,
and were doing before we came, and if possible help them to do
it better. Some Jesuit missionaries in China are actually sent to
remote villages and required to earn their living there by the
practice of an indigenous craft for at least two years before they
are allowed to teach at all. Some such condition as this ought
to be imposed upon all foreign teachers, whether in mission or
government schools. How dare we forget that we are dealing
with peoples "whose intellectual interests are the same from the
top of the social structure to the bottom," and for whom our
unfortunate distinctions of religious from secular learning, fine
from applied art, and significance from use have not yet been
made? When we have introduced these distinctions and have
divided an "educated" from a still "illiterate" class, it is to the
latter that we must turn if we want to study the language, the
poetry, and the whole culture of these peoples, "before it is too
late."

In speaking of a "proselytizing fury" in a former article I
had not only in view the activities of professed missionaries but
more generally those of everyone bent by the weight of the
white man's burden and anxious to confer the "blessings" of
our civilization upon others. What lies below this fury, of which
our punitive expeditions and "wars of pacification" are only
more evident manifestations? It would not be too much to say

that our educational activities abroad (a word that must be taken to include the American Indian reservations) are motivated by an *intention* to destroy existing cultures. And that is not only, I think, because of our conviction of the absolute superiority of our *Kultur,* and consequent contempt and hatred for whatever else we have not understood (all those for whom the economic motive is not decisive), but grounded in an unconscious and deep-rooted envy of the serenity and leisure that we cannot help but recognize in people whom we call "unspoiled." It irks us that these others, who are neither, as we are, industrialized nor, as we are, "democratic," should nevertheless be *contented;* we feel bound to discontent them, and especially to discontent their women, who might learn from us to work in factories or to find careers. I used the word *Kultur* deliberately just now, because there is not much real difference between the Germans' will to enforce their culture upon the backward races of the rest of Europe and our determination to enforce our own upon the rest of the world; the methods employed in their case may be more evidently brutal, but the kind of will involved is the same.[20] As I implied above, that "misery loves company" is the true and unacknowledged basis of our will to create a brave new world of uniformly literate mechanics. This was recently repeated to a group of young American workmen, one of whom responded, "And *are* we miserable!"

But however we may be whistling in the dark when we pride ourselves upon "the collective wisdom of a literate people," regardless of what is read by the "literates," the primary concern of the present essay is not with the limitations and defects of modern Western education *in situ,* but with the spread of an education of this type elsewhere. Our real concern is with the fallacy involved in the attachment of an absolute value to literacy, and the very dangerous consequences that are involved in the setting up of "literacy" as a standard by which to measure the cultures of unlettered peoples. Our blind faith in literacy not only obscures for us the significance of other skills, so that we care not under what subhuman conditions a man may have to learn his living, if only he can read, no matter what, in his hours of leisure; it is also one of the fundamental grounds of interracial prejudice and becomes a prime factor in the spiritual impoverishment of all the "backward" people whom we propose to "civilize."

REFERENCES

[1] *Metaphysics,* VI: 2, 4, and XI: 8, 12. "Reading, for a man devoid of prior-understanding, is like a blind man's looking in a mirror" (*Garuḍa Purāṇa,* XVI: 82).

[2] Walter Shewring, "Literacy," in the *Dictionary of World Literature,* 1943. "We are becoming culturally illiterate faster than all these agencies are managing to make us literate in the use of the potentialities of the culture" (Robert S. Lynd, in *Knowledge for What?*). Professor John U. Nef of Chicago, speaking at Hamline University in 1944, remarked: "In spite of the alleged great spread of literacy [in America] . . . the proportion of the population who can communicate with each other on a relatively high level of discourse is very much smaller than it was." A recent study sponsored by the Carnegie Foundation for the Advancement of Teaching found that "the average senior in six colleges recognized only 61 out of 100 words in familiar use by educated people"! In view of all the facts, it is indeed astonishing to find Lord Raglan saying: "By savage I mean illiterate" (in the *Rationalist Annual,* 1946, p. 43). There was a time, indeed, when the English bourgeoisie thought of the Gaelic Highlanders as "savages"; but from an anthropologist one would expect a refutation of such "myths," rather than their revival!

[3] F. G. Childe, *English and Scottish Popular Ballads,* Introduction by G. L. Kittredge. Cf. W. W. Comfort, *Chrétien de Troyes* (Everyman's Library), Introduction: Chrétien's poetry "was intended for a society that was still homogeneous, and to it at the outset doubtless all classes of the population listened with equal interest." Nothing of this kind is or can be achieved by the organized and compulsory education of today—"a province of its own, detached from life" with its

THE BUGBEAR OF LITERACY

"atmosphere of intense boredom that damps the vitality of the young" and of which "the result is: the young people do not know anything really well," or as "it would be more exact to say, they do not know what knowledge is," which "explains the dangerous gullibility which propaganda exploits" (Erich Meissner, *Germany in Peril*, 1942, pp. 47, 48).

[4] Douglas Hyde, *Literary History of Ireland*, 1903, p. 633.

[5] American is already "a one-dimensional public language, a language oriented to the description of external aspects of behavior, weak in overtones . . . our words lack . . . the formal precision which comes from awareness of past and different usage" (Margaret Mead, *And Keep Your Powder Dry*, 1942, p. 82). Any author who uses words precisely is liable to be misunderstood.

"Perhaps at no other time have men been so knowing and yet so unaware, so burdened with purposes and so purposeless, so disillusioned and so completely the victims of illusion. This strange contradiction pervades our entire modern culture, our science and our philosophy, our literature and our art" (W. M. Urban, *The Intelligible World*, 1929, p. 172). Under such conditions, ability to read a printed page becomes a mere trick, and is no guarantee whatever of power to grasp or to communicate ideas.

[6] Robert Knox, *An Historical Relation of Ceylon*, 1681 (1911 ed., p. 168).

[7] J. F. Campbell, *Popular Tales of the West Highlands* (1890 ed., pp. v, xxiii, cxxii).

[8] Alexander Carmichael, *Carmina Gadelica*, Vol. I, 1900, pp. xxiii, xxix. Cf. J. G. Mackay, *More West Highland Tales*, 1940, General Preface: "The poorest classes generally speak the language admirably. . . . Some recited thousands of lines of ancient heroic poems. . . . Another cause of the fragmentary character of some tales is the obliterating effect of modern civilisation"; and J. Watson, *ibid.*, Introduction: "This intellectual inheritance . . . this ancient culture extended over all the north and northerly midlands of Scotland. The people who possessed this culture may have been, and usually were, unlettered. They were far from being uneducated. It is sad to think that its decay has been partly due to the schools and the Church!" It is, in fact, precisely by "the schools and the Church" that the decay of cultures all over the world has been hastened in the last hundred years.

H. J. Massingham in *This Plot of Earth* (1944, p. 233) tells of "the old man, Seonardh Coinbeul, who could neither read nor write and carried 4500 lines of his own bardic composition in his head, together with all manner of songs and stories."

A. Solonylsin in the *Asiatic Review* (NS. XLI, Jan., 1945, p. 86) remarks that the recording of the Kirghiz epic is still incomplete, although over 1,100,000 lines have already been taken down by the Kirghiz Research Institute—"Bards who recite the 'Manas'—or 'Manaschi'—have phenomenal memories in addition to poetic talent. Only this can explain the fact that hundreds of thousands of verses have been handed down orally." A writer reviewing *Manas, Kirghiski Narodni Epos* in the *Journal of American Folklore*, 58, 1945, p. 65, observes that "general education has already done much to remove the raison d'être of the minstrel's position in tribal life. . . . With acculturation becoming a rolling Juggernaut it is not surprising that what remains of epic singing may soon degenerate into an artificial and ostentatiously national publicity device."

[9] R. St. Barbe Baker, *Africa Drums*, 1942, p. 145.

[10] W. G. Archer, *The Blue Grove*, 1940, Preface; and in JBORS, Vol. XXIX, p. 68.

[11] Edward Schröder Prior and Arthur Gardner, *An Account of Medieval Figure-Sculpture in England*, 1912, p. 25.

[12] Paul Radin, *Primitive Man as Philosopher*, 1927.

[13] J. Strzygowski, *Spüren indogermanische Glaubens in der bildenden Kunst*, 1936, p. 344.

[14] Tom Harrisson, *Savage Civilisation*, 1937, pp. 45, 344, 351, 353.

[15] Plato, *Phaedrus*, 275 f. Cf. H. Gauss, *Plato's Conception of Philosophy*, 1937, pp. 262-5.

[16] Sir George A. Grierson, *Lallā Vākyāni*, 1920, p. 3.

[17] Albert Schweitzer, *On the Edge of the Primeval Forest*.

[18] *De reductione artium ad theologiam*, 14.

[19] N. K. Chadwick, *Poetry and Prophecy*, 1942, Preface, further, "The experience of exclusively literate communities is too narrow." "Ever learning, and never able to come to the knowledge of the truth" (II Timothy 3:7)!

[20] Modern "education" imposed upon traditional cultures (e.g. Gaelic, Indian, Polynesian, American Indian) is only less deliberately,

not less actually, destructive than the Nazi destruction of Polish libraries, which was intended to wipe out their racial memories; the Germans acted consciously, but we who Anglicize or Americanize or Frenchify are driven by a rancor that we do not recognize and could not confess. This rancor is, in fact, our reaction to a superiority that we resent and therefore would like to destroy.

Chapter III

PATHS THAT LEAD TO THE SAME SUMMIT

"There is no Natural Religion. . . . As all men are alike (though infinitely various), so all Religions, as all similars, have one source"—William Blake

"There is but one salvation for all mankind, and that is the life of God in the soul."—William Law

THE constant increase of contacts between ourselves, who for the purposes of the present essay may be assumed to be Christians, and other peoples who belong to the great non-Christian majority has made it more than ever before an urgent necessity for us to understand the faiths by which they live. Such an understanding is at the same time intrinsically to be desired, and indispensable for the solution by agreement of the economic and political problems by which the peoples of the world are at present more divided than united. We cannot establish human relationships with other peoples if we are convinced of our own superiority or superior wisdom, and only want to convert them to our way of thinking. The modern Christian, who thinks of the world as his parish, is faced with the painful necessity of becoming himself a citizen of the world; he is invited to participate in a symposium and a *convivium;* not to preside—for there is Another who presides unseen—but as one of many guests.

It is no longer only for the professed missionary that a study of other religions than his own is required. This very essay, for example, is based upon an address given to a large group of schoolteachers in a series entitled "How to Teach about Other Peoples," sponsored by the New York School Board and the East and West Association. It has, too, been proposed that in all the schools and universities of the postwar world stress should be laid on the teaching of the basic principles of the great world religions as a means of promoting international understanding and developing a concept of world citizenship.

The question next arises, By whom can such teaching be properly given? It will be self-evident that no one can have understood, and so be qualified to teach, a religion, who is opposed to all religion; this will rule out the rationalist and scientific humanist, and ultimately all those whose conception of religion is not theological, but merely ethical. The obvious ideal would be for the great religions to be taught only by those who confess them; but this is an ideal that could only be realized, for the present, in our larger universities. It has been proposed to establish a school of this kind at Oxford.

As things are, a teaching about other than Christian faiths is mainly given in theological seminaries and missionary colleges by men who do believe that Christianity is the only true faith, who approve of foreign missions, and who wish to prepare the missionary for his work. Under these conditions, the study of comparative religion necessarily assumes a character quite different from that of other disciplines; it cannot but be biased. It is obvious that if we are to teach at all it should be our intention to communicate only truth: but where a teaching takes for granted that the subject matter to be dealt with is intrinsically of inferior significance, and the subject is taught, not *con amore,* but only to instruct the future schoolmaster in the problems that he will have to cope with, one cannot but suspect that at least a part of the truth will be suppressed, if not intentionally, at least unknowingly.

If comparative religion is to be taught as other sciences are taught, the teacher must surely have recognized that his own religion is only one of those that are to be "compared"; he may not expound any "pet theories" of his own, but is to present the truth without bias, to the extent that it lies in his power. In other words, it will be "necessary to recognize that those institutions which are based on the same premises, let us say the supernatural, must be considered together, our own amongst the rest," whereas "today, whether it is a question of imperialism, or of race prejudice, or of a comparison between Christianity and paganism, we are still preoccupied with the uniqueness . . . of our own institutions and achievements, our own civilization." [1] One cannot but ask whether the Christian whose conviction is ineradicable that his is the only true faith can conscientiously permit himself to expound another religion, knowing that he cannot do so honestly.

We are, then, in proposing to teach about other peoples, faced with the problem of tolerance. The word is not a pretty one; to tolerate is to put up with, endure, or suffer the existence of what are or appear to be other ways of thinking than our own; and it is neither very pleasant merely "to put up with" our neighbors and fellow guests, nor very pleasant to feel that one's own deepest institutions and beliefs are being patiently "endured." Moreover, if the Western world is actually more tolerant today than it was some centuries ago, or has been since the fall of Rome, it is largely because men are no longer sure that there is any truth of which we can be certain, and are inclined to the "democratic" belief that one man's opinion is as good as another's, especially in the fields of politics, art, and religion. Tolerance, then, is a merely negative virtue, demanding no sacrifice of spiritual pride and involving no abrogation of our sense of superiority; it can be commended only in so far as it means that we shall refrain from hating or persecuting others who differ or seem to differ from ourselves in habit or belief. Tolerance still allows us to pity those who differ from ourselves, and are consequently to be pitied!

Tolerance, carried further, implies indifference, and becomes intolerable. Our proposal is not that we should tolerate heresies, but rather come to some agreement about the truth. Our proposition is that the proper objective of an education in comparative religion should be to enable the pupil to discuss with other believers the validity of particular doctrines,[2] leaving the problem of the truth or falsity, superiority or inferiority, of whole bodies of doctrine in abeyance until we have had at least an opportunity to know in what respects they really differ from one another, and whether in essentials or in accidentals. We take it for granted, of course, that they will inevitably differ accidentally, since "nothing can be known except in the mode of the knower." One must at least have been taught to recognize equivalent symbols, e.g., rose and lotus (Rosa Mundi and Padmāvatī); that Soma is the "bread and water of life"; or that the Maker of all things is by no means accidentally, but necessárily a "carpenter" wherever the material of which the world is made is *hylic*. The proposed objective has this further and immediate advantage, that it is not in conflict with even the most rigid Christian orthodoxy; it has never been denied that some truths are embodied in the pagan beliefs, and even St. Thomas Aquinas was ready and willing to find in the works of the pagan philosophers "extrinsic and probable proofs" of the truths of Christianity. He was, indeed, acquainted only with the ancients and with the Jews and some Arabians; but there is no reason why the modern Christian, if his mental equipment is adequate, should not learn to recognize or be delighted to find in, let us say, Vedāntic, Sūfī, Taoist, or American Indian formulations extrinsic and probable proofs of the truth as he knows it. It is more than probable, indeed, that his contacts with other believers will be of very great advantage to the Christian student in his exegesis and understanding of Christian doctrine; for though himself a believer, this is in spite of the nominalist intellectual environment in which he was born and bred, and by which he cannot but be to some degree affected; while the Oriental (to whom the miracles attributed to Christ present no problem) is still a realist, born and bred in a realistic environment, and is therefore in a position to approach Plato or St. John, Dante or Meister Eckhart more simply and directly than the Western scholar who cannot but have been affected to some extent by the doubts and difficulties that force themselves upon those whose education and environment have been for the greater part profane.

Such a procedure as we have suggested provides us immediately with a basis for a common understanding and for co-operation. What we have in view is an ultimate "reunion of the churches" in a far wider sense than that in which this expression is commonly employed: the substitution of active alliances—let us say of Christianity and Hinduism or Islam, on the basis of commonly recognized first principles, and with a view to an effective co-operation in the application of these principles to the contingent fields of art (manufacture) and prudence—for what is at present nothing better than a civil war between the members of one human family, children of one and the same God, "whom," as Philo said, *with one accord* all Greeks and Barbarians acknowledge together." [3] It is with reference to this statement that Professor Goodenough remarks that, "So far as I can see Philo was telling the simple truth about paganism as he saw it, not as Christian propaganda has ever since misrepresented it."

It need not be concealed that such alliances will necessarily involve an abandonment of all missionary enterprises such as they are now; interdenominational conferences will take the place of those proselytizing expeditions of which the only permanent result is the secularization and destruction of existing cultures and the pulling up of individuals by their roots. *You* have already reached the point at which culture and religion, utility and meaning, have been divorced and can be considered apart, but this is not true of those peoples whom you propose to convert, whose religion and culture *are one and the same thing* and none of the functions of whose life are necessarily profane or unprincipled. If ever you should succeed in persuading the Hindus that their revealed scriptures are valid only "as literature," you will have reduced them to the level of your own college men who read the Bible, if at all, only as literature. Christianity in India, as Sister Nivedita (Patrick Geddes' distinguished pupil, and author of *The Web of Indian Life*) once remarked, "carries drunkenness in its wake"[4]—for if you teach a man that what he has thought right is wrong, he will be apt to think that what he has thought wrong is right.

We are all alike in need of repentance and conversion, a "change of mind" and a "turning round": not, however, from one *form* of belief to another, but from unbelief to belief. There can be no more vicious kind of tolerance than to approach another man, to tell him that "We are both serving the same God, you in your way and I in His!" The "compassing of sea and land to make one proselyte" can be carried on as an institution only for so long as our ignorance of other peoples' faiths persists. The subsidizing of educational or medical services accessory to the primary purpose of conversion is a form of simony and an infringement of the instruction, "Heal the sick . . . provide neither gold nor silver nor brass in your purses, nor scrip for your journey . . . [but go] forth as sheep in the midst of wolves." Wherever you go, it must be not as masters or superiors but as guests, or as we might say nowadays, "exchange professors"; you must not return to betray the confidences of your hosts by any libel. Your vocation must be purged of any notion of a "civilizing mission"; for what you think of as "the white man's burden" here is a matter of "white shadows in the South Seas" there. Your "Christian" civilization is ending in disaster—and you are bold enough to offer it to others! Realize that, as Professor Plumer has said, "the surest way to betray our Chinese allies is to sell, give or lend-lease them our [American] standard of living,"[5] and that the hardest task you could undertake for the present and immediate future is to friend of mine, in correspondence, speaks of Srī Ramakrishna as convince the Orient that the civilization of Europe is in any sense a Christian civilization, or that there really are reasonable, just, and tolerable Europeans amongst the "barbarians" of whom the Orient lives in terror.

The word "heresy" means choice, the having opinions of one's own, and thinking what we *like* to think: we can only grasp its real meaning today, when "thinking for oneself" is so highly recommended (with the proviso that the thinking must be "100 per cent"), if we realize that the modern equivalent of heresy is "treason." The one outstanding, and perhaps the only, real heresy of modern Christianity in the eyes of other believers is its claim to exclusive truth; for this is treason against Him who "never left himself without a witness," and can only be paralleled by Peter's denial of Christ; and whoever says to his pagan friends that "the light that is in you is darkness," in offending these is offending the Father of lights. In view of St. Ambrose's well-known gloss on I Corinthians 12:3, "all that is true, *by whomsoever it has been said,* is from the Holy Ghost" (a dictum endorsed by St. Thomas Aquinas), you may be asked, "On what grounds do you propose to distinguish between your own 'revealed' religion and our 'natural' religion, for which, in fact, we also claim a supernatural origin?" You may find this question hard to answer.

The claim to an exclusive validity is by no means calculated to make for the survival of Christianity in a world prepared to prove all things. On the contrary, it may weaken enormously its prestige in relation to other traditions in which a very different attitude prevails, and which are under no necessity of engaging in any polemic. As a great German theologian has said, "human culture [*Menschheitsbildung*] is a unitary whole, and its separate cultures are the dialects of one and the same language of the spirit." [6] The quarrel of Christianity with other religions seems to an Oriental as much a tactical error in the conflict of ideal with sensate motivations as it would have been for the Allies to turn against the Chinese on the battlefield. Nor will he participate in such a quarrel; much rather he will say, what I have often said to Christian friends, "Even if you are not on our side, we are on yours." The converse attitude is rarely expressed; but twice in my life I have met a Roman Catholic who could freely admit that for a Hindu to become a professing Christian was not essential to salvation. Yet, could we believe it, the Truth or Justice with which we are all alike and unconditionally concerned is like the Round Table to which "al the worlde crysten and hethen repayren" to eat of one and the same bread and drink the same wine, and at which "all are equal, the high and the low." A very learned Roman Catholic friend of mine, in correspondence, speaks of Śrī Rāmakrishna as "another Christ . . . Christ's own self."

Let us now, for a moment, consider the points of view that have been expressed by the ancients and other non-Christians when they speak of religions other than their own. We have already quoted Philo. Plutarch, first with bitter irony disposing of the Greek euhemerists "who spread atheism all over the world by obliterating the Gods of our belief and turning them all alike into the names of generals, admirals and kings," and of the Greeks who could no longer distinguish Apollo (the intelligible Sun) from Helios (the sensible sun), goes on to say: "Nor do we speak of the 'different Gods' of different peoples, or of the

Gods as 'Barbarian' and 'Greek,' but as common to all, though differently named by different peoples, so that for the One Reason (Logos) that orders all these things, and the One Providence that oversees them, and for the minor powers [i.e., gods, angels] that are appointed to care for all things, there have arisen among different peoples different epithets and services, according to their different manners and customs."[7] Apuleius recognizes that the Egyptian Isis (our Mother Nature and Madonna, Natura Naturans, Creatrix, Deus) "is adored throughout the world in divers manners, in variable customs and by many names."[8]

The Mussulman Emperor of India, Jahāngīr, writing of his friend and teacher, the Hindu hermit Jadrūp, says that "his Vedānta is the same as our Tasawwuf":[9] and, in fact, Northern India abounds in a type of religious literature in which it is often difficult, if not impossible, to distinguish Mussulman from Hindu factors. The indifference of religious forms is indeed, as Professor Nicholson remarks, "a cardinal Sūfī doctrine." So we find ibn-ul-'Arabī saying:

> My heart is capable of every form: it is a pasture for
>   gazelles and a convent for Christian monks,
> And idol-temple and the pilgrim's Ka'ba [Mecca], and
>   the tables of the Torah and the book of the Koran;
> I follow the religion of Love, whichever way his camels
>   take; my religion and my faith is the true religion.[10]

That is to say that you and I, whose religions are distinguishable, can each of us say that "mine is the true religion," *and* to one another that "yours is the true religion"—whether or not either or both of us be truly religious depending not upon the form of our religion but upon ourselves and on grace. So, too, Shams-i-Tabriz:

If the notion of my Beloved is to be found in an idol-
temple,
'Twere mortal sin to circumscribe the Ka'ba!
The Ka'ba is but a church if there His trace be lost:
My Ka'ba is whatever "church" in which His trace
is found! [11]

Similarly in Hinduism; the Tamil poet-saint Tāyumānavar,
for example, says in a hymn to Śiva:

Thou didst fittingly . . . inspire as Teacher millions
of religions.
Thou didst in each religion, while it like the rest
showed in splendid fulness of treatises, disputa-
tions, sciences, [make] each its tenet to be the
truth, the final goal.[12]

The *Bhaktakalpadruma* of Pratāpa Siṁha maintains that
"every man should, as far as in him lieth, help the reading of
the Scriptures, whether those of his own church or those of
another." [13]

In the *Bhagavad Gītā* (VII, 21) Śrī Krishna proclaims: "If
any lover whatsoever seeks with faith to worship any form
[of God] whatever, it is I who am the founder of his faith,"
and (IV, 11), "However men approach Me, even do I reward
them, for the path men take from every side is Mine." [14]

We have the word of Christ himself that he came to call,
not the just, but sinners (Matthew 9:13). What can we make
out of that, but that, as St. Justin said, "God is the Word of
whom the whole human race are partakers, and those who lived
according to Reason are Christians even though accounted
atheists. . . . Socrates and Heracleitus, and of the barbarians
Abraham and many others." So, too, Meister Eckhart, greatest of the Christian mystics, speaks of Plato (whom the Moslem Jīlī saw in a vision, "filling the world with light") as

"that great priest," and as having "found the way ere ever Christ was born." Was St. Augustine wrong when he affirmed that "the very thing that is now called the Christian religion was not wanting amongst the ancients from the beginning of the human race, until Christ came in the flesh, after which the true religion, which already existed, began to be called 'Christian' "? Had he not retracted these brave words, the bloodstained history of Christianity might have been otherwise written!

We have come to think of religion more as a set of rules of conduct than as a doctrine about God; less as a doctrine about what we should *be,* than one of what we ought to *do;* and because there is necessarily an element of contingency in every application of principles to particular cases, we have come to believe that theory differs as practice must. This confusion of necessary means with transcendent ends (as if the vision of God could be earned by works) has had unfortunate results for Christianity, both at home and abroad. The more the Church has devoted herself to "social service," the more her influence has declined; an age that regards monasticism as an almost immoral retreat is itself unarmed. It is mainly because religion has been offered to modern men in nauseatingly sentimental terms ("Be good, sweet child," etc.), and no longer as an intellectual challenge, that so many have been revolted, thinking that *that* "is all there is to" religion. Such an emphasis on ethics (and, incidentally, forgetfulness that Christian doctrine has as much to do with art, i.e. manufacture, making, what and how, as it has to do with behavior) plays into the skeptic's hands; for the desirability and convenience of the social virtues is such and so evident that it is felt that if that *is* all that religion means, why bring in a God to sanction forms of conduct of which no one denies the propriety? Why indeed? [15] At the same time this excessive emphasis upon the moral, and neglect of the intellectual virtues (which last alone, in orthodox Christian teaching, are held to survive our dissolution) invite the retorts of the rationalists who maintain that religion has never been anything but a means of drugging the lower classes and keeping them quiet.

Against all that, the severe intellectual discipline that any serious study of Eastern, or even "primitive," religion and philosophy demands can serve as a useful corrective. The task of co-operation in the field of comparative religion is one that demands the highest possible qualifications; if we cannot give our best to the task, it would be safer not to undertake it. The time is fast coming when it will be as necessary for the man who is to be called "educated" to know either Arabic, Sanskrit, or Chinese as it is now for him to read Latin, Greek, or Hebrew. And this, above all, in the case of those who are to teach about other peoples' faiths; for existing translations are often in many different ways inadequate, and if we are to know whether or not it is true that all believing men have hitherto worshiped and still worship one and the same God, whether by his English, Latin, Arabic, Chinese, or Navajo names, one must have searched the scriptures of the world—never forgetting that *sine desiderio mens non intelligit*.

Nor may we undertake these activities of instruction with ulterior motives: as in all other educational activities, so here the teacher's effort must be directed to the interest and advantage of the pupil himself, not that he may do good, but that he may be good. The dictum that "charity begins at home" is by no means necessarily a cynicism: it rather takes for granted that to do good is only possible when we are good, and that if we are good we shall do good, whether by action or inaction, speech or silence. It is sound Christian doctrine that a man must first have known and loved himself, his inner man, before he loves his neighbor.

It is, then, the pupil who comes first in our conception of the teaching of comparative religion. He will be astounded by the effect upon his understanding of Christian doctrine that can be induced by the recognition of similar doctrines stated in another language and by means of what are to him strange or even grotesque figures of thought. In the following of the *vestigia pedis,* the soul "in hot pursuit of her quarry, Christ," he will recognize an idiom of the language of the spirit that has come down to us from the hunting cultures of the Stone Age; a cannibal philosophy in that of the Eucharist and the Soma sacrifice; and the doctrine of the "seven rays" of the intelligible Sun in that of the Seven Gifts of the Spirit and in the "seven eyes" of the Apocalyptic Lamb and of Cuchulainn. He may find himself far less inclined than he is now to recoil from Christ's harder sayings, or those of St. Paul on the "sundering of soul from spirit." If he balks at the command to hate, not merely his earthly relatives, but "yea, and his own soul also," and prefers the milder wording of the Authorized Version, where "life" replaces "soul," or if he would like to interpret in a merely ethical sense the command to "deny himself," although the word that is rendered by "deny" means "utterly reject"; if he now begins to realize that the "soul" is of the dust that returns to the dust when the spirit returns to God who gave it, and that equally for Hebrew and Arabic theologians this "soul" *(nefesh, nafs)* imports that carnal "individuality" of which the Christian mystics are thinking when they say that "the soul must put itself to death"; or that our existence (distinguishing *esse* from *essentia,* γένεσις from οὐσία, *bhū* from *as*) is a crime; and if he correlates all these ideas with the Islamic and Indian exhortation to "die before you die" and with St. Paul's "I live, yet *not I,*" then he may be less inclined to read into Christian doctrine any promise of eternal life for any "soul" that has been concreated with the body—and better equipped to show that the spiritualists' "proofs" of the survival of human personality, however valid, have no religious bearings whatever.

The mind of the democratic student to whom the very name of the concept of a "divine right" may be unintelligible is likely to be roughly awakened if he ever realizes that, as Professor Buckler often reminds us, the very notion of a *kingdom* of God on earth "depends for its revelation on the inner meaning of eastern kingship," for he may have forgotten in his righteous detestation of all dictatorships, that the classical definition of "tyranny" is that of "a king ruling in his own interests."

Nor is this a one-sided transaction; it would not be easy to exaggerate the alteration that can be brought about in the Hindu's or Buddhist's estimate of Christianity when the opportunity is given him to come into closer contact with the quality of thought that led Vincent of Beauvais to speak of Christ's "ferocity" and Dante to marvel at "the multitude of teeth with which this Love bites."

"Some contemplate one Name, and some another? Which of these is the best? All are eminent clues to the transcendent, immortal, unembodied Brahma: these Names are to be contemplated, lauded, and at last denied. For by them one rises higher and higher in these worlds; but where all comes to its end, there he attains to the Unity of the Person" *(Maitri Upanishad)*. Whoever knows this text, but nothing of Western technique, will assuredly be moved by a sympathetic understanding when he learns that the Christian also follows a *via affirmativa* and a *via remotionis!* Whoever has been taught a doctrine of "liberation from the pairs of opposites" (past and future, pleasure and pain, etc., the Symplegades of "folklore") will be stirred by Nicholas of Cusa's description of the wall of Paradise wherein God dwells as "built of contradictories," and by Dante's of what lies beyond this wall as "not in space, nor hath it poles," but "where every where and every when is focussed." We all need to realize, with Xenophon, that "when God is our teacher, we come to think alike."

For there are as many of these Hindus and Buddhists whose knowledge of Christianity and of the greatest Christian writers is virtually nil, as there are Christians, equally learned, whose real knowledge of any other religion but their own is virtually nil, because they have never imagined what it might be to *live* these other faiths. Just as there can be no real knowledge of a language if we have never even imaginatively participated in the activities to which the language refers, so there can be no real knowledge of any "life" that one has not in some measure lived. The greatest of modern Indian saints actually practiced Christian and Islamic disciplines, that is, worshiped Christ and Allah, and found that all led to the same goal: he could speak from experience of the equal validity of all these "ways," and feel the same respect for each, while still preferring for himself the one to which his whole being was naturally attuned by nativity, temperament, and training. What a loss it would have been to his countrymen and to the world, and even to Christianity, if he had "become a Christian"! There are many paths that lead to the summit of one and the same mountain; their differences will be the more apparent the lower down we are, but they vanish at the peak; each will naturally take the one that starts from the point at which he finds himself; he who goes round about the mountain looking for another is not climbing. Never let us approach another believer to ask him to become "one of *us*," but approach him with respect as one who is already "one of *His*," who *is*, and from whose invariable beauty all contingent being depends! [16]

REFERENCES

[1] Ruth Benedict, *Patterns of Culture*, 1934, p. 5.

[2] To illustrate what I mean by "discussion" here, I refer the reader to my article entitled, "On Being in One's Right Mind," in the *Review of Religion*, Vol. VII, New York, 1942, pp. 32-40. Although in fact by one author, this article is in effect a collaboration of Christian, Platonist, and Hindu, expounding a doctrine held in common.

[3] Philo Judaeus, *De specialibus legibus* II, 65; E. R. Goodenough, *Introduction to Philo Judaeus*, 1940, pp. 105, 108.

[4] *Lambs among Wolves*, 1903. See also my "Christian Missions in India" in *Essays in National Idealism* (1st ed., 1909; or 2nd ed.).

[5] J. M. Plumer, "China's High Standard of Living," *Asia and the Americas* February, 1944.

[6] Alfred Jeremias, *Altorientalische Geisteskultur*, Vorwort. "A long metaphysical chain runs throughout the world and connects all races" (Johannes Sauter, in *Archiv für Rechts- und Sozialphilosophie*, Berlin, October, 1934).

[7] Plutarch, *Isis and Osiris*, 67 (*Moralia*, 377). So William Law, in continuation of the citation above, "There is not one [salvation] for the Jew, another for the Christian, and a third for the heathen. No, God is one, human nature is one, and the way to it is one; and that is, the desire of the soul turned to God." Actually, this refers to "the baptism of desire," or "of the Spirit" (as distinguished from baptism by water, which involves an actual membership in the Christian community) and only modifies the Christian dogma *extra Ecclesiam nulla salus*. The real problem is that of the proper meaning of the words "Catholic Church"; we say that this should mean not any one religion as such, but the community, or universe of experience, of all those who love God. As William Law says also: "The chief hurt of a sect is this, that it takes itself to be necessary to the truth, whereas the truth is only then found when it is known to be of no sect but as free and universal as the goodness of God and as common to all names and nations as the air and light of this world."

Cf. F. W. Buckler: "The layman, Dissenter, schismatic or the heathen, who wittingly or unwittingly has taken up his Cross, is a child of the kingdom of God on earth and a *Khalīfah* of our Lord, as the priest or bishop, who has not taken up his Cross, however unquestionable his Apostolic continuity, is not" (*The Epiphany of the Cross*, 1938). It should also be borne in mind that (as the last mentioned author has often shown) the Christian concept of the "kingdom of God" cannot be properly understood except in the light of the Oriental theory of Kingship and Divine Right.

[8] Apuleius, *Golden Ass*, XI, 5.

Cf. Alfred Jeremias, *Der Kosmos von Sumer* (*Der Alte Orient*, 32, Leipzig, 1932), Ch. III, "*Die eine Madonna.*"

[9] *Tūzuk-i-Jahāngīrī* (Memoirs of Jahāngīr), in the version by Rogers and Beveridge, 1905, p. 356.

[10] R. A. Nicholson, *Mystics of Islam*, 1914, p. 105. Similarly, "If he [the follower of any particular religion] understood the saying of Junayd, 'The color of the water is the color of the water containing it,' he would not interfere with the beliefs of others, but would perceive God in every form and in every belief" (ibn-ul-'Arabī, Nicholson, *Studies in Islamic Mysticism*, 1921, p. 159). And, "Henceforth I knew that there were not many gods of human worship, but one God only, who was polyonomous and polymorphous, being figured and named according to the variety of the outward condition of things" (Sir George Birdwood, *Sva*, 1915, p. 28).

[11] R. A. Nicholson, *Diwānī Shams-i-Tabrīz*, 1898, p. 238, cf. 221.

Cf. Farīdu'd Dīn 'Aṭṭār, in the *Manṭiqu't Ṭayr:* "Since, then, there are different ways of making the journey, no two [soul-] birds will fly alike. Each finds a way of his own, on this road of mystic knowledge, one by means of the Mihrāb, and another through the Idol."

[12] Sir P. Arunachalam, *Studies and Translations*, Colombo, 1937, p. 201.

[13] Translation by Sir George Grierson, *JRAS*, 1908, p. 347.

[14] Schleiermacher rightly maintains (*Reden*, V) that the multiplicity of religions is grounded in the nature of religion itself, and necessary for its complete manifestation—"*Nur in der Totalität aller solcher möglichen Formen kann die ganze Religion wirklich gegeben werden.*" But Schleiermacher claims the highest position for Christianity—on the grounds of its freedom from exclusiveness!

Una veritas in variis signis varie resplendeat: and in the words of Marsilio Ficino, "Perhaps, indeed, this kind of variety, ordained by God himself, displays a certain admirable adornment of the universe" (*De christiana religione*, c. 4).

Cf. also Ernest Cassirer's exposition of Pico della Mirandola's "defence of the *libertas credendi*," in the *Journal of the History of Ideas*, III, 335.

[15] The answer can be given in the words of Christopher Dawson: "For when once morality has been deprived of its religious and metaphysical foundations, it inevitably becomes subordinated to lower ends." As he also says, the need for a restoration of the ethics of vocation has become the central problem of society—"vocation" being that station of life to which it has pleased God to call us, and not the "job" to which our own ambitions drive.

[16] The following books are commended to the reader's attention:

Sister Nivedita, *Lambs among Wolves* (1903) and *The Web of Indian Life* (1904 or later editions)

Demetra Vaka, *Haremlik* (1911)

Paul Radin, *Primitive Man as Philosopher* (1927)

Father W. Schmidt, *The High Gods of North America* (1933) and *Origin and Growth of Religion* (2nd ed., 1935)

Lord Raglan, *The Hero* (1936)

Aldous Huxley, *Ends and Means* (1937); *The Perennial Philosophy* (1945); *Science, Liberty, and Peace* (1946)

René Guénon, *East and West* (1941); *Crisis of the Modern World* (1942); *General Introduction to the Hindu Doctrines* (1946)

Marco Pallis, *Peaks and Lamas* (1941)

R. St. Barbe Baker, *Africa Drums* (1942)

Swami Nikhilananda, *The Gospel of Sri Ramakrishna* (1942)

N. K. Chadwick, *Poetry and Prophecy* (1942)

A. K. Coomaraswamy, *Hinduism and Buddhism* (1943); *The Religious Basis of the Forms of Indian Society* (1946)

Sir P. Arunachalam, *Studies and Translations* (1937)

Sir George Birdwood, *Sva* (1915)

J. C. Archer, *The Sikhs* (1946)

Chapter IV

EASTERN WISDOM AND WESTERN KNOWLEDGE

East and West, The Crisis of the Modern World, Introduction to the Study of the Hindu Doctrines, and *Man and His Becoming* (Luzac, London, 1941–46) are the first of a series in which the majority of René Guénon's works already published in French will appear in English. Another version of *Man and His Becoming* had appeared earlier.[1] M. René Guénon is not an "Orientalist" but what the Hindus would call a "master," formerly resident in Paris, and now for many years in Egypt, where his affiliations are Islamic. His *Introduction genérale à l'étude des doctrines hindoues* appeared in 1921.[2] As a preliminary to his further expositions of the traditional philosophy, sometimes called the *Philosophia Perennis* (*et Universalis* must be understood, for this "philosophy" has been the common inheritance of all mankind without exception), Guénon cleared the ground of all possible misconception in two large and rather tedious, but by no means unnecessary, volumes,. *L'Erreur spirite* (i.e. "Fallacy of Spiritualism," a work for which *Bhagavad Gītā,* XVII, 4, "Men of darkness are they who make a cult of the departed and of spirits," might have served as a motto),[3] and *Le Theosophisme, histoire d'une pseudo-religion.*[4] These are followed by *L'Homme et son devenir selon le Vedanta* and *L'Esotérisme de Dante,*[5] *Le roi du monde,*[6] *St. Bernard,*[7] *Orient et Occident* and *Autorité spirituelle et pouvoir temporel,*[8] *Le symbolisme de la croix,*[9] *Les états multiples de l'être,*[10] and *La métaphysique orientale.*[11] More recently M. Guénon has published in mimeographed, and subsequently printed, editions *Le règne de la quantité et les signes des temps* [12] and *Les principes du calcul infinitésimal*.[13]

In the meantime important articles from Guénon's pen appeared monthly in *La Voile d'Isis*, later *Études Traditionnelles*, a journal of which the appearance was interrupted by the war, but which has been continued as from September-October, 1945. *Études Traditionnelles* is devoted to *"La Tradition Perpétuelle et Unanime, révélée tant par les dogmes et les rites des religions orthodoxes que par la.langue universelle des symboles initiatiques."* Of articles that have appeared elsewhere attention may be called to *"L'Esotérisme Islamique"* in *Cahiers du Sud*.[14] Excerpts from Guénon's writings, with some comment, have appeared in *Triveni* (1935) and in the *Viśvabharatī Quarterly* (1935, 1938). A work by L. de Gaigneron entitled *Vers la connaissance interdite* [15] is closely connected with Guénon's; it is presented in the form of a discussion in which the Ātman (Spiritus), Mentalié ("Reason," in the current, not the Platonic, sense), and a Roman abbé take part; the "forbidden knowledge" is that of the gnosis which the modern Church and the rationalist alike reject, though for very different reasons—the former because it cannot tolerate a point of view which considers Christianity only as one amongst other orthodox religions and the latter because, as a great Orientalist (Professor A. B. Keith) has remarked, "such knowledge as is not empirical is meaningless to us and should not be described as knowledge" [16]—an almost classical confession of the limitations of the "scientific" position.

Guénon's French is at once precise and limpid, and inevitably loses in translation; his subject matter is of absorbing interest, at least to anyone who cares for what Plato calls the really serious things.[17] Nevertheless it has often been found unpalatable; partly for reasons already given, but also for reasons that have been stated, paradoxically enough, by a reviewer of Blakney's *Meister Eckhart* in the *Harvard Divinity School Bul-*

letin,[18] who says that "To an age which believes in personality
and personalism, the impersonality of mysticism is baffling; and
to an age which is trying to quicken its insight into history the
indifference of the mystics to events in time is disconcerting."
As for history, Guénon's "he who cannot escape from the standpoint of temporal succession so as to see all things in their
simultaneity is incapable of the least conception of the metaphysical order"[19] adequately complements Jacob Behmen's
designation of the "history that was once brought to pass" as
"merely the (outward) form of Christianity."[20] For the Hindu,
the events of the Ṛgveda are nowever and dateless, and the
Krishna Līlā "not an historical event"; and the reliance of
Christianity upon supposedly historical "facts" seems to be its
greatest weakness. The value of literary history for doxography
is very little, and it is for this reason that so many orthodox
Hindus have thought of Western scholarship as a "crime":
their interest is not in "what men have believed," but in the
truth. A further difficulty is presented by Guénon's uncom-
promising language; "Western civilization is an anomaly, not
to say a monstrosity." Of this a reviewer[21] has remarked that
"such sweeping remarks cannot be shared even by critics of
Western achievements." I should have thought that now that
its denouement is before our eyes, the truth of such a statement
might have been recognized by every unprejudiced European;
at any rate Sir George Birdwood in 1915 described modern
Western civilization as "secular, joyless, inane, and self-destructive" and Professor La Piana has said that "what we call our
civilization is but a murderous machine with no conscience and
no ideals"[22] and might well have said suicidal as well as murderous. It would be very easy to cite innumerable criticisms of
the same kind; Sir S. Radhakrishnan holds, for example, that
"civilization is not worth saving if it continues on its present
foundations,"[23] and this it would be hard to deny; Professor

A. N. Whitehead has spoken quite as forcibly—"There remains the show of civilization, without any of its realities."[24]

In any case, if we are to read Guénon at all, we must have outgrown the temporally provincial view that has for so long and so complacently envisaged a continuous progress of humanity culminating in the twentieth century and be willing at least to ask ourselves whether there has not been rather a continued decline, "from the stone age until now," as one of the most learned men in the U.S.A. once put it to me. It is not by "science" that we can be saved: "the possession of the sciences as a whole, if it does not include the best, will in some few cases aid but more often harm the owner."[25] "We are obliged to admit that our European culture is a culture of the mind and senses only";[26] "The prostitution of science may lead to world catastrophe";[27] "Our dignity and our interests require that we shall be the directors and not the victims of technical and scientific advance";[28] "Few will deny that the twentieth century thus far has brought us bitter disappointment."[29] "We are now faced with the prospect of complete bankruptcy in every department of life."[30] Eric Gill speaks of the "monstrous inhumanity" of industrialism, and of the modern way of life, as "neither human nor normal nor Christian. . . . It is our way of thinking that is odd and unnatural."[31] This sense of frustration is perhaps the most encouraging sign of the times. We have laid stress on these things because it is only to those who feel this frustration, and not to those who still believe in progress, that Guénon addresses himself; to those who are complacent everything that he has to say will seem to be preposterous.

The reactions of Roman Catholics to Guénon are illuminating. One has pointed out that he is a "serious metaphysician," i.e. one convinced of the truth he expounds and eager to show the unanimity of the Eastern and scholastic traditions, and observes that "in such matters belief and understanding must go together." [32] *Crede ut intelligas* is a piece of advice that modern scholars would, indeed, do well to consider; it is, perhaps, just because we have not believed that we have not yet understood the East. The same author writes of *East and West*, "René Guénon is one of the few writers of our time whose work is really of importance . . . he stands for the primacy of pure metaphysics over all other forms of knowledge, and presents himself as the exponent of a major tradition of thought, predominantly Eastern, but shared in the Middle Ages by the scholastics of the West . . . clearly Guénon's position is not that of Christian orthodoxy, but many, perhaps most, of his theses are, in fact, better in accord with authentic Thomist doctrine than are many opinions of devout but ill-instructed Christians." [33] We should do well to remember that even St. Thomas Aquinas did not disdain to make use of "intrinsic and probable proofs" derived from the "pagan" philosophers.

Gerald Vann, on the other hand, makes the mistake which the title of his review, "René Guénon's Orientalism," [34] announces; for this is not another "ism," nor a geographical antithesis, but one of modern empiricism and traditional theory. Vann springs to the defense of the very Christianity in which Guénon himself sees almost the only possibility of salvation for the West; only possibility, not because there is no other body of truth, but because the mentality of the West is adapted to and needs a religion of just this sort. But if Christianity should fail, it is just because its intellectual aspects have been submerged, and it has become a code of ethics rather than a doctrine from which all other applications can and should be derived; hardly two consecutive sentences of some of Meister Eckhart's sermons would be intelligible to an average modern congregation, which does not expect doctrine, and only expects to be told how to behave. If Guénon wants the West to turn

to Eastern metaphysics, it is not because they are Eastern but
because this *is* metaphysics. If "Eastern" metaphysics differed
from a "Western" metaphysics—as true philosophy differs
from what is often so called in our modern universities—one or
the other would not be metaphysics. It is from metaphysics that
the West has turned away in its desperate endeavor to live by
bread alone, an endeavor of which the Dead Sea fruits are before
our eyes. It is only because this metaphysics still survives as a
living power in Eastern societies, in so far as they have not been
corrupted by the withering touch of Western, or rather, *modern*
civilization (for the contrast is not of East or West as such, but
of "those paths that the rest of mankind follows as a matter
of course" with those post-Renaissance paths that have brought
us to our present impasse), and not to Orientalize the West,
but to bring back the West to a consciousness of the roots of
her own life and of values that have been transvalued in the
most sinister sense, that Guénon asks us to turn to the East.
He does not mean, and makes it very clear that he does not
mean, that Europeans ought to become Hindus or Buddhists,
but much rather that they, who are getting nowhere by the
study of "the Bible as literature," or that of Dante "as a poet,"
should rediscover Christianity, or what amounts to the same
thing, Plato ("that great priest," as Meister Eckhart calls him).
I often marvel at men's immunity to the *Apology* and *Phaedo*
or the seventh chapter of the *Republic;* I suppose it is because
they would not hear, "though one rose from the dead."

The issue of "East and West" is not merely a theoretical
(we must remind the modern reader that from the standpoint
of the traditional philosophy, "theoretical" is anything but a
term of disparagement) but also an urgent practical problem.
Pearl Buck asks, "Why should prejudices be so strong at this
moment? The answer it seems to me is simple. Physical con-
veyance and other circumstances have forced parts of the world

once remote from each other into actual intimacy for which peoples are *not mentally or spiritually prepared*. . . . It is not necessary to believe that this initial stage must continue. If those prepared to act as interpreters will do their proper work, we may find that within another generation or two, or even sooner, dislike and prejudice may be gone. This is only possible if prompt and strong measures are taken by peoples to keep step mentally with the increasing closeness to which the war is compelling us." [35] But if this is to happen, the West will have to abandon what Guénon calls its "proselytizing fury," an expression that must *not* be taken to refer only to the activities of Christian missionaries, regrettable as these often are, but to those of all the distributors of modern "civilization" and those of practically all those "educators" who feel that they have more to give than to learn from what are often called the "backward" or "unprogressive" peoples; to whom it does not occur that one may not wish or need to "progress" if one has reached a state of equilibrium that already provides for the realization of what one regards as the greatest purposes of life. It is as an expression of good will and of the best intentions that this proselytizing fury takes on its most dangerous aspects. To many this "fury" can only suggest the fable of the fox that lost its tail, and persuaded the other foxes to cut off theirs. An industrialization of the East may be inevitable, but do not let us call it a blessing that a folk should be reduced to the level of a proletariat, or assume that materially higher standards of living necessarily make for greater happiness. The West is only just discovering, to its great astonishment, that "material inducements, that is, money or the things that money can buy" are by no means so cogent a force as has been supposed; "Beyond the subsistence level, the theory that this incentive is decisive is largely an illusion." [36] As for the East, as Guénon says, "The only impression that, for example, mechanical inventions make on most Orientals is one of deep repulsion; certainly it all seems to them far more harmful than beneficial, and if they find themselves obliged to accept certain things which the present epoch has made necessary, they do so in the hope of future riddance . . . what the people of the West call 'rising' would be called by some 'sinking'; that is what all true Orientals think." [87] It must not be supposed that because so many Eastern peoples have imitated us in self-defense that they have therefore accepted our values; on the contrary, it is just because the conservative East still challenges all the presuppositions on which our illusion of progress rests, that it deserves our most serious consideration.

There is nothing in economic intimacies that is likely to reduce prejudice or promote mutual understandings automatically. Even when Europeans live amongst Orientals, *"economic contact between the Eastern and Western groups is practically the only contact there is. There is very little social or religious give and take between the two. Each lives in a world almost entirely closed to the other—and by 'closed' we mean not only 'unknown' but more: incomprehensible and unattainable."* [88] That is an inhuman relationship, by which both parties are degraded.

Neither must it be assumed that the Orient thinks it important that the masses should learn to read and write. Literacy is a practical necessity in an industrial society, where the keeping of accounts is all important. But in India, in so far as Western methods of education have not been imposed from without, all higher education is imparted orally, and to have *heard* is far more important than to have *read*. At the same time the peasant, prevented by his illiteracy and poverty from devouring the newspapers and magazines that form the daily and almost the only reading of the vast majority of Western "literates," is, like Hesiod's Boeotian farmers, and still more like the Gaelic-speaking Highlanders before the era of the board schools, thoroughly

familiar with an epic literature of profound spiritual significance
and a body of poetry and music of incalculable value; and one
can only regret the spread of an "education" that involves the
destruction of all these things, or only preserves them as curi-
osities within the covers of books. For cultural purposes it is
not important that the masses should be literate; it is not necessary that anyone should be literate; it is only necessary that
there should be amongst the people philosophers (in the traditional, not the modern sense of the word), and that there should
be preserved deep respect on the part of laymen for true learning that is the antithesis of the American attitude to a "professor." In these respects the whole East is still far in advance
of the West, and hence the learning of the elite exerts a far
profounder influence upon society as a whole than the Western
specialist "thinker" can ever hope to wield.

It is not, however, primarily with a protection of the East
against the subversive inroads of Western "culture" that Guénon is concerned, but rather with the question, What possibility of regeneration, if any, can be envisaged for the West?
The possibility exists only in the event of a return to first
principles and to the normal ways of living that proceed from
the application of first principles to contingent circumstances;
and as it is only in the East that these things are still alive, it
is to the East that the West must turn. "It is the West that
must take the initiative, but she must be prepared really to go
towards the East, not merely seeking to draw the East towards
herself, as she has tried to do so far. There is no reason why
the East should take this initiative, and there would still be
none, even if the Western world were not in such a state as
to make any effort in this direction useless. . . . It now remains
for us to show how the West might attempt to approach the
East." [39]

He proceeds to show that the work is to be done in the two

fields of metaphysics and religion, and that it can only be carried out on the highest intellectual levels, where agreement on first principles can be reached and apart from any propaganda on behalf of or even apology for "Western civilization."

The work must be undertaken, therefore, by an "elite." And as it is here more than anywhere that Guénon's meaning is likely to be willfully misinterpreted, we must understand clearly what he means by such an elite. The divergence of the West and East being only "accidental," "the bringing of these two portions of mankind together and the return of the West to a normal civilization are really just one and the same thing." An elite will necessarily work in the first place "for itself, since its members will naturally reap from their own development an immediate and altogether unfailing benefit." An indirect result—"indirect," because on this intellectual level one does not think of "doing good" to others, or in terms of "service," but seeks truth because one needs it oneself—would, or might under favorable conditions, bring about "a return of the West to a traditional civilization," i.e. one in which "everything is seen as the application and extension of a doctrine whose essence is purely intellectual and metaphysical." [40]

It is emphasized again and again that such an elite does not mean a body of specialists or scholars who would absorb and put over on the West the forms of an alien culture, nor even persuade the West to return to such a traditional civilization as existed in the Middle Ages. Traditional cultures develop by the application of principles to conditions; the principles, indeed, are unchangeable and universal, but just as nothing can be known except in the mode of the knower, so nothing valid can be accomplished socially without taking into account the character of those concerned and the particular circumstances of the period in which they live. There is no "fusion" of cultures to be hoped for; it would be nothing like an "eclecticism" or "syncretism" that an elite would have in view. Neither would such an elite be organized in any way so as to exercise such a direct influence as that which, for example, the Technocrats would like to exercise for the good of mankind. If such an elite ever came into being, the vast majority of Western men would never know of it; it would operate only as a sort of leaven, and certainly on behalf of rather than against whatever survives of traditional essence in, for example, the Greek Orthodox and Roman Catholic domains. It is, indeed, a curious fact that some of the most powerful defenders of Christian dogma are to be found amongst Orientals who are not themselves Christians, or ever likely to become Christians, but recognize in the Christian tradition an embodiment of the universal truth to which God has never nor anywhere left himself without a witness.

In the meantime, M. Guénon asks, "Is this really 'the beginning of an end' for the modern civilization? . . . At least there are many signs which should give food for reflection to those who are still capable of it; will the West be able to regain control of herself in time?" Few would deny that we are faced with the possibility of a total disintegration of culture. We are at war with ourselves, and *therefore* at war with one another. Western man is unbalanced, and the question, Can he recover himself? is a very real one. No one to whom the question presents itself can afford to ignore the writings of the leading living exponent of a traditional wisdom that is no more essentially Oriental than it is Occidental, though it may be only in the uttermost parts of the earth that it is still remembered and must be sought.

REFERENCES

[1] London, Rider, 1928.
[2] Paris, 2nd ed., 1932.
[3] Paris, 1923, 2nd ed., 1930.
[4] Paris, 1921, 2nd ed., 1930.

[5] Both Paris, 1925.

[6] Paris, 1927.

[7] Marseille, 1929.

[8] Both Paris, 1930.

[9] Paris, 1931.

[10] Paris, 1932.

[11] Paris, 1939—a lecture delivered at the Sorbonne in 1925; 2nd ed. 1946.

[12] Cairo, 1943, and London, 1944.

[13] Cairo, 1943. Printed Paris, 1946.

[14] 22me année, 1935.

[15] Paris, 1935.

[16] *Aitareya Āraṇyaka*, Oxford, 1909, p. 42.

[17] *Laws*, 803 B, C; *Philebus*, 58 A; *Republic*, 521 C, D; *Timaeus*, 47 B, etc.

[18] XXXIX, 1942, p. 107.

[19] *La métaphysique orientale*, p. 17.

[20] *Signatura rerum*, XV, 24.

[21] Betty Heiman in *BSOAS.*, X, 1942, p. 1048.

[22] *Harvard Divinity School Bulletin*, XXVII, 27.

[23] *Eastern Religions and Western Thought*, p. 257.

[24] *Adventures of Ideas*, 1933, p. 358.

[25] Plato, *Alcibiades*, II, 144 D.

[26] Worrington, *Form in Gothic*, p. 75.

[27] Leroy Waterman in *JAOS*, LVIII, 410.

[28] Rt. Hon. Herbert Morison in the British Association Report, *Science and World Order*, January, 1942, p. 33.

[29] Professor J. M. Mecklin in *Passing of the Saint*, p. 197.

[30] Lionel Giles in *Luzac's Oriental List*.

[31] *Autobiography*, pp. 145, 174, 279.

[32] Walter Shewring in the *Weekly Review*, January, 1939.

[33] *Weekly Review*, August 28, 1941.

[34] In the *New English Weekly*, September, 1941.

[35] *Asia*, March, 1942, italics mine.

[36] National Research Council, *Fatigue of Workers*, 1942, p. 143.

[37] *East and West*, pp. 44, 71.

[38] J. H. Boeke, *Structure of Netherlands Indian Economy*, 1942, p. 68.

[39] *East and West*, p. 162.

[40] *East and West*, p. 241.

Chapter V

EAST AND WEST

"EAST and West" imports a cultural rather than a geographical antithesis: an opposition of the traditional or ordinary way of life that survives in the East to the modern and irregular way of life that now prevails in the West. It is because such an opposition as this could not have been felt before the Renaissance that we say that the problem is one that presents itself only accidentally in terms of geography; it is one of times much more than of places. For if we leave out of account the "modernistic" and individual philosophies of today, and consider only the great tradition of the magnanimous philosophers, whose philosophy was also a religion that had to be lived if it was to be understood, it will soon be found that the distinctions of cultures in East and West, or for that matter North and South, are comparable only to those of dialects; all are speaking what is essentially one and the same spiritual language, employing different words, but expressing the same ideas, and very often by means of identical idioms. Otherwise stated, there is a universally intelligible language, not only verbal but also visual, of the fundamental ideas on which the different civilizations have been founded.

There exists, then, in this commonly accepted axiology or body of first principles a common universe of discourse; and this provides us with the necessary basis for communication, understanding, and agreement, and so for effective co-operation in the application of commonly recognized spiritual values to the solution of contingent problems of organization and conduct. It is clear, however, that all this understanding and agree-

ment can be reached and verified only by philosophers or
scholars, if such are to be found, who are more than philologues
and to whom their knowledge of the great tradition has been
a vital and transforming experience; of such is the leaven or
ferment by which the epigonous and decaying civilizations of
today might be "renewed in knowledge." I quote St Paul's
"in knowledge," not with reference to a knowledge of the
"facts of science" or any power to "conquer nature," but as
referring to the knowledge of our Self which the true philosophers of East and West alike have always considered the *sine
qua non* of wisdom; and because this is not a matter of anyone's "illiteracy" or ignorance of "facts," but one of the restoration of meaning or value to a world of "impoverished reality."
East and West are at cross-purposes only because the West is
determined, i.e. at once resolved and economically "determined," to keep on going it knows not where, and calls this
rudderless voyage (see the woodcut by Eric Gill, facing p. 1)
"progress."

It is far more, of course, by what our ideal philosophers and
scholars, functioning as mediators, might *be,* far more by the
simple fact of their presence, as of a catalyst, than by any kind
of intervention in political or economic activities that they could
operate effectively; they would have no use for votes or wish
to "represent" their several nations at Geneva; and remaining
unseen, they could arouse no opposition. At the present moment
I can think of only two or three of this kind: René Guénon,
Frithiof Schuon, Marco Pallis; one cannot consider from this
point of view those who know only the West or only the East,
however well.

On the other hand, no mere good will or philanthropy will
suffice; and while it is true that correct solutions will necessarily
be good ones, it by no means follows that what to the altruist
seems to be good will also be right. There is no room here for

the proselytizing fury of any "idealists." What "the century of the common man" actually predicates is the century of the economic man, the economically determined man whose best and worst are equally unprincipled—a man who is far too common for our ends. How many of our "communists," I wonder, realize that the reference of "the common man," *communis homo,* was originally not to the man in the street as such, but to the immanent deity, the very Man in everyman! In the meantime, what "free enterprise" means is "his hand—the common man's in our sense—against every man's, and every man's hand against him": and there lie the fertile seeds of future wars. What we demand is something other than a quantitative standard of living; a form of society in which, in the words of St. Augustine, "everyone has his divinely coordinated place, and his security, and honour, and content therein; and no one is envious of another's high estate, and reverence, and happiness; where God is sought, and is found, and is magnified in everything"; one in which, in the words of Pius XII, "all work has an inherent dignity and at the same time a close connection with the perfection of the person"—an almost literal summary of the true philosophy of work as it has been propounded by Plato and in the *Bhagavad Gītā.* I know of no form of society in which such a condition has been more nearly realized than the Indian, of which the late Sir George Birdwood, himself a convinced and exemplary Christian, said that "such an ideal order we should have held impossible of realisation, but that it continues to exist [however precariously], and to afford us, in the yet living results of its daily operation in India, a proof of the superiority, in so many unsuspected ways, of the hieratic civilisation of antiquity over the secular, joyless, inane, and self-destructive civilisation of the West."

We have got to reckon with the fact that almost all Western

nations are either feared or hated and distrusted by almost all
Eastern peoples, and to ask ourselves why this should be so, and
whether the former are unchangeably of such a sort as to seem
to be destroyers everywhere, makers of deserts and calling them
peace. Already in 1761 William Law asked men to "look at
all European Christendom sailing round the globe with fire and
sword and every murdering art of war to seize the possessions
and kill the inhabitants of both the Indies. What natural right
of man, what supernatural virtue, which Christ brought down
from Heaven, was not here trodden under foot? All that you
have ever read or heard of heathen barbarity was here outdone
by Christian conquerors. And to this day, what wars of Christians against Christians . . . for a miserable share in the spoils
of a plundered heathen world." Written immediately after
a year of British military triumphs "in every quarter of the
world," these words, like those of the concluding chapters of
Gulliver's Travels, might have been written twenty years ago
when the news of the Amritsar massacre had first leaked out,
or today when it is officially admitted that since the beginning
of the present war British soldiers have repeatedly fired on unarmed crowds, when flogging is a common punishment for
political offenses, and thousands of elected representatives and
other "political offenders" (most of them committed to the
employment of only "nonviolent" means) have been long in
prison without charge or trial, and no man knows when he may
not be arrested and detained incommunicado in the same way.
And all that because "the loss of India would consummate the
downfall of the British Empire," and the British Government,
the "Holdfast" (Namuci—the Indian Fafnir, or "Pharaoh" as
described in Ezekiel 29:3) of the present age means to "hold its
own" ill-gotten gains in the name of a "moral responsibility"
to peoples who may have been divided against themselves
(divide et impera), but are certainly not divided in wanting

to be freed to solve their own difficulties. It is no wonder that the heathen rage; not in their "blindness," but because they see only too clearly that empire is a commercial-financial institution having theft as its final object.[1]

But politics and economics, although they cannot be ignored, are the most external and the least part of our problem; it is not through them that understanding and agreement can be reached, but on the contrary through understanding that the political and economic problems can be solved. The first spiritual problem in the solution of which there must be a co-operation (if we are thinking of anything better than a mere imposition of our own manners and customs on other peoples), and with respect to which a common theory has been entertained, is that of the elimination of the profit motive by which capital and labor are nowadays equally dominated and inhibited. In other words, the problem is that of the restoration of the concept of vocation, not as a matter of arbitrary "choice," or of passive determination by monetary needs or social ambition, but of occupations to which one is imperiously summoned by one's own nature and in which, accordingly, every man can be working out at the same time the perfection of his product and his own entelechy. For it is inevitably true that in this way, as Plato says, "more will be done, and better done, and more easily than in any other way," a proposition of which the command, "Seek first the kingdom of God and his righteousness" (δικαιοσύνη=*dharma*), and the promise that "all these things shall be added unto you," is an almost literal paraphrase.

In a vocational order it is assumed that every trade (i.e. "walk" of life) is appropriate to someone, and consonant with human dignity; and this means in the final analysis, that if there are any occupations that are *not* consistent with human dignity, or any things intrinsically worthless, such occupations and manufactures must be abandoned by a society that has in view the dignity of all its members. This is, then, the problem of the use and abuse of machines: use, if the instrument enables the workman to make well what is needed and in the making of which he can delight, or abuse if the instrument, in which some other party has a vested interest opposed to the workman's own, itself controls the kind and quality of his product. The distinction is that of the tool (however complicated) that helps the man to make the thing he wants to make, from the machine (however simple) that must be served by the man whom it, in fact, controls. This is a problem that must be solved if the world is to be made "safe for democracy" and safe from exploitation; and that can be solved by agreement only when the *intentions* of the traditional "caste" systems have been understood, and it has been fully realized that these intentions can never be fulfilled within the framework of a capitalist industrialism, however "democratic," and can only be fulfilled where production is primarily "for good use." Nor is this a matter to be regarded only from the producer's point of view; there are values also from a consumer's point of view, and who is not a consumer? It must be recognized (the proofs are ready to hand in any good museum) that machines, as defined above, are not the equivalent of tools, but substitutes for tools, and that whatever is made by such machines directly for human use is qualitatively inferior to what can be made with the help of tools. I have observed the standing advertisement of a dealer in used carpets; up to $50 is offered for "Americans" and up to $500 for "Orientals." It is ultimately for the consumer to decide whether he wants to live on a $50 or a $500 level; and no society organized upon the basis of "the law of the sharks" can expect to do the latter. The combination of quality with quantity is a chimera in the likeness of the service of God and Mammon, and equally impossible. Where we shall *not* be able to agree is in thinking that "wealth" or "high standards of living" can be measured in terms of quantity and competitive pricing.

Failing an understanding and agreement on the higher levels of reference, there is the imminent danger that in bringing forth a brave new world in which all men shall fraternize, this may amount to nothing more than, if even to so much as, that they may eat, drink, and be merry together in the intervals of the so-called peace that occasionally interrupts the wars of acquisition, pacification, and education. The work of "missionaries," whether of a given religion, of scientific humanism, or industrialism, is a leveling rather than an elevating force, fundamentally incompatible with anything but a reduction of the cultures of the world to their lowest common denominator— "Father, forgive them; for they know not what they do!" Merely to have set up elsewhere replicas of the modern institutions in which the West for the most part still believes, although these are the very ways of living that have already bred disaster, merely to dream of mixing the oil of "economic justice" with the acid of a competitive "world trade," is not enough for felicity; the backward East, in so far as it is still "backward," is very much happier, calmer, and less afraid of life and death than the "forward" West has ever been or can be. To have set about to "conquer" nature, to have thought of discontent as "divine," to have honored the discoverers of "new wants," [2] to have sacrificed spontaneity to the concept of an inevitable "progress" [3]— these positions of the "Social Gospel" are none of those that the East has ever thought of as making for happiness.

It emerges from what has been said above that motion toward a *rapprochement* must originate in the West; if only because it is the modern West that first abandoned the once common norms, while the surviving East that is still in a majority, however diminished and diminishing, still adheres to them. It is true that there is another and modernized, uprooted

East, with which the West can *compete*: but it is only with the surviving, the super-stitious East—Gandhi's East, the one that has never attempted to live by bread alone—that the West can *co-operate*. Who knows this East? It is from our philosophers, scholars, and theologians that we have a right to expect such a knowledge; and it is actually, in the first place, upon our Western universities and churches, our "educators," that the responsibility of the future of international relations rests, however little they are presently and really able to play their part in "dissipating the clouds of ignorance which hide the East from the West." We need scholars (and that in the pulpit, in college classrooms, and "on the air") to whom not only Latin and Greek, but also Arabic or Persian, Sanskrit or Tamil, and Chinese or Tibetan are still living languages in the sense that there are to be found formulations of principles pertinent to all men's lives; we need translators, bearing in mind that to translate without betrayal one must have experienced oneself the content that is to be "carried across." We need theologians who can think no more or less in terms of Christian than of Islamic, Hindu or Taoist theology, and who have realized by a personal verification that, as Philo said, all men "whether Greeks or barbarians" actually recognize and serve one and the same God, by whatever names, or, if you prefer it, one and the same immanent "Son of Man," the Son of whom Meister Eckhart spoke when he said that "he who sees *me, sees my child*." We need anthropologists of the caliber of Richard St. Barbe Baker, Karl von Spiess, Father W. Schmidt, and Nora K. Chadwick and such folklorists as were the late J. F. Campbell and Alexander Carmichael—the value of such men as the late Professor A. A. Macdonell and Sir J. G. Frazer being only that of hewers of wood and drawers of water for those who "understand their material."

We need mediators to whom the common universe of discourse is still a reality, men of a sort that is rarely bred in public schools or trained in modern universities; and this means that the primary problem is that of the re-education of Western literati.[4] More than one has told me how it had taken him ten years to outgrow even a Harvard education; I have no idea how many it might take to outgrow a missionary college education, or to recover from a course of lectures on comparative religion offered by a Calvinist. We need "reactionaries," able to start over again from scratch—from an *in principio* in the logical rather than any temporal sense, and very surely not merely in the *ante quo bellum* sense, the point at which the education of the amnesic "common man" of today begins. I mean by "reactionaries" men who, when an impasse has been reached, are not afraid of being told that "we cannot put back the hands of the clock" or that "the machine has come to stay." The real intention of my reactionaries, for whom there is no such thing as a "dead past," is not to put back the hands but to put them forward to another noonday. We need men who are not afraid of being told that "human nature is unchangeable"; which is true enough in its proper sense, but not if we are under the delusion that human nature is nothing but an economic nature. What should we think of a man who has lost his way and reached the brink of a precipice—and is it not "down a steep place into the sea" that European civilization, for all its possibly good intentions, is gliding now?—and is too stupid or too proud to retrace his steps? Who, indeed, would not now retrace his steps, if he only knew how! The proof of this can be seen in the multiplicity of the current "plans" for a better world that men pursue, never remembering that there is only "one thing needful." The modern West must be "renewed—in knowledge."

Again, we must beware; for there are two possible, and very different, consequences that can follow from the cultural contact of East and West. One can, like Jawaharlal Nehru, and in his own words, "become a queer mixture of East and West, out of place everywhere, at home nowhere"; *or*, being still oneself, one can learn to find oneself "in place" anywhere, and "at home" everywhere—in the profoundest sense, a citizen of the world.

The problem is "educational," or in other words, one of "recollection"; and when it has been solved, when the West has found herself again—the Self of all other men—the problem of understanding the "mysterious" East will have been solved at the same time, and nothing will remain but the practical task of putting into practice what has been remembered. The alternative is that of a reduction of the whole world to the present state of Europe. The choice lies finally between a deliberately directed movement toward a foreseen goal or "destiny," and a passive submission to an inexorable progress or "fate"; between an evaluated and significant and a valueless and insignificant way of living.

REFERENCES

[1] "It is very proper that in England a good share of the produce of the earth should be appropriated to support certain families in affluence, to produce senators, sages and heroes for the service and defense of the state . . . *but in India,* that haughty spirit, *independence and deep thought,* which the possession of great wealth sometimes gives, *ought to be suppressed. They are directly adverse to our political power*" (*Skeen Commission Report,* H. M. Stationery Office, London; and London *Times,* August, 1927, p. 9)—italics mine.

Such frank cynicism is infinitely preferable to the sentimentality of those who wonder why the people of India are not "grateful" for all the benefits that British rule has conferred upon them. The British civil servant, paid with Indian money, has no right to devote himself to anything but the good of India; he may or may not be personally lovable, but his work is nothing but his duty, which, if well done, should earn respect, but hardly gratitude. But "foreign rule is a ter-

rible curse and the minor benefits it may confer can never compensate
for the spiritual degradation it involves" (*Hindustan Times*, November 25, 1945).

[2] "The common factor of the whole situation lies in the simple
facts that at any given period the material requirements of the individual are quite definitely limited—that any attempt to expand them
artificially is an interference with the plain trend of evolution, which
is to subordinate material to mental and psychological necessity; and
that the impulse behind unbridled industrialism is not progressive
but reactionary" (Douglas, *Economic Democracy*, 1918, quoted in
Lionel Birch, *The Waggoner on the Footplate*, 1933, p. 130). "The
best virtues of a nation nearly always begin to disappear when mutual obligations are converted into money values, because the sense of
partnership and obligation becomes lost in a welter of legal without
moral contract. It is not unfair to say that the villein of the Middle
Ages was a freer man and had more security and dignity of status
than the wage-slave of to-day. This aspect has been overlooked and
denied by the Whig historians who genuinely believed in the glories
of laissez-faire and in the spiritual beauties of 'devil take the hindmost' " (Earl of Portsmouth, *Alternative to Death*, 1944, p. 87).

[3] "*Dans l'Inde chaque occupation est un sacerdoce. . . . Les métiers
et les rites ne peuvent se distinguer exactement et le mot Sanskrit
karma, 'action,' 'oeuvre,' s'applique aux deux. . . . On peut chasser
un mercenaire mais non un serviteur héréditaire. Donc pour récolter
la tranquillité et un bon service, il faut user de tact et de bonnes
manières. Le service héréditaire est tout à fait incompatible avec
l'industrialisme actuel et c'est pourquoi il est peint sous des couleurs
aussi sombres*" (A. M. Hocart, *Les castes*, 1938, pp. 27, 28, 238).
"The most potent factor [in the illusion called Progress], however,
was the triumph of Mammon in the industrial revolution, which
disorganised the Church, created a new feudalism, and reduced the
son of man once more to servitude, this time to a machine and a
machine-made law. The effect of the last phase is illustrated by the
stress the nineteenth century has laid on punctuality as a virtue, not
as a matter of consideration for the convenience of others but because an employer could not be expected to keep a machine waiting
for any man—'the son of man.' He became a cog in the great
machine, while to the industrialist, the Holy Spirit, whose divinity
he recognized, was steam. . . . Has the Church, through all her

vicissitudes, retained sufficient of our Lord's teaching and triumph to restore 'the son of man' to his due—to be seated on the right hand of power?" (F. W. Buckler, *The Epiphany of the Cross*, 1938, pp. 64, 69.)

[4] "And if our unconscious nationalistic prejudices have thus prevented any significant philosophical cooperation in this limited [i.e. European] area, still more completely has our Occidental superiority complex (which apparently dominates philosophers as much as other people) blocked any genuine cooperation between Western and Eastern thinkers. We just presuppose as a matter of course that all tenable solutions of all real problems can or will be found in the Western tradition.

"This smug and Pharisaic complacency is one of the causes of war; it is also a factor in other causes. And it is the cause that philosophers are primarily responsible to remove. They can remove it only by acquiring a deep and persistent interest in other philosophical perspectives than their own, especially those in Latin America, Russia, China, and India. Such an interest will express itself in the expansion of philosophy departments to include teachers of these subjects; in increased travel on the part of philosophers, aided by the establishment of visiting fellowships and exchange professorships; and in more general mastery of the necessary linguistic tools" (E. A. Burtt in *The Journal of Philosophy*, 42, 1945, p. 490).

Chapter VI

"SPIRITUAL PATERNITY"
AND THE "PUPPET COMPLEX"

*These are really the thoughts of all men in all ages and
lands, they are not original with me. If they are not yours
as much as mine, they are nothing, or next to nothing.—
Walt Whitman*

THE purpose of this chapter is methodological, and mainly
to suggest that the anthropologist is rather too much inclined
to consider the pecularities of "primitive" people—*Naturvölker*
—in isolation, neglecting the possibility or probability that
these peculiarities may not be of local origin, but may represent
only provincial or peripheral survivals of theories held by some
or all of the more sophisticated communities from which the
primitive peoples may have declined.

The first example will be that of the belief of some Pacific
and Australian peoples in a spiritual paternity. The subject is
so well known to anthropologists that it will suffice to cite from
a recent article by Dr. M. F. Ashley Montagu,[1] who remarks
that "practically everywhere in Australia . . . intercourse is
associated with conception, *but not as a cause of conception or
childbirth.*[2] . . . The belief is rather that a spirit-child has
entered into her . . . it is the *official doctrine* of spiritual conception that looms largely in their thinking . . . intercourse
serves to *prepare* the woman for the entry of the spirit-child."
Further, with reference to Roheim's data, Professor Montagu
remarks that "it would seem probable that until the native is
initiated into the social interpretation of the nature of things he
is under the impression that intercourse is closely connected with
childbirth; when, however, he has been initiated into the *tra-*

ditional teachings he discovers his former elementary knowledge to have been incomplete, and he gradually shifts the emphasis from a belief in material reproduction to one in favour of spiritual reproduction."

In these citations mark the words "associated with . . . but not as a cause," "official doctrine," and "traditional teachings." Before we proceed further it should be noted that it is evidence of a rather considerable intellectual development to be able to distinguish a *post hoc* from a *propter hoc,* concomitance from causation. Nor is this by any means the only available evidence of the "intellectuality" of the Australian aborigines. But are they any more likely than any other peoples to have invented, in any datable sense, their own "official doctrines"? Or should an explanation of such phenomena as the universality of the Symplegades motive be sought in the notion of the "common denominator"? One might as well try to account for the cognate forms of words in related languages as try to explain the distribution of cognate ideas in that way!

The Pacific doctrine of spiritual conception is anything but an isolated phenomenon. For example, it is explicitly stated in the Buddhist canonical literature that three things are necessary for conception: the union of father and mother, the mother's period, *and the presence of the Gandharva*[3]—the divine and solar Eros. The *Gandharva* here corresponds to the divine Nature that Philo calls "the highest, elder and true cause" of generation, while the parents are merely concomitant causes;[4] and to Plato's "ever-productive Nature"[5] and to St. Paul's "Father" *ex quo omnis paternitas in coelis et terra nominatur.*[6] It would be difficult to distinguish these formulations from that of the Australian aborigines with their initiatory "official doctrine" in which sexual intercourse is associated with conception, but not as its cause. It would be equally difficult to distinguish the Australian from Aristotle's doctrine that

"Man and the Sun [7] generate man," [8] or from Dante's designation of the Sun,[7] a pregnant light, as "the father of each mortal life," whose reglowing rays enable each to say, *Subsisto.*[9] These formulations, in turn, correspond to those of the *Śatapatha Brāhmaṇa* where it is inasmuch as they are "kissed," that is breathed upon, by the Sun [7] that each of the children of men can say "I am" (*asmi*) or, in the Commentator's words, "acquires a self." [10] Again, the Australian distinction of the mediate from the first cause of conception is closely paralleled in the *Jaiminīya Upaniṣad Brāhmaṇa:* "When the [human] father thus emits him as seed into the womb, it is really the Sun [7] that emits him as seed into the womb . . . thence is he born, after that seed, that Breath." [11] One cannot, indeed, distinguish him "who puts the seed in plants, in cows, in mares and in women" [12] from Dante's "Sun," or from the "fertility spirit" of the "primitives."

In greater detail, "Say not, 'From semen,' but 'from what is alive' [therein]"; [13] that is, "He who, present in [*tiṣṭhan = instans*] the semen, whom the semen knoweth not . . . whose body [vehicle] the semen is , . . the Immortal"; [14] "it is that prescient-spiritual-Self [*prajñātman,* the Sun] [15] that grasps and erects the flesh." [16] This, or in other words that "Light is the progenitive power" [17] are familiar Christian doctrines. "Present in the semen," for example, has its equivalent in St. Thomas Aquinas: "The power of the soul, which is in the semen through the Spirit enclosed therein, fashions the body," [18] and so "the power of generation belongs to God," [19] and in the words of Schiller, *"Es ist der Geist der sich den Körper schaft."* [20]

Similarly, St. Bonaventura wrote: *"Generatio non potest fieri in materia generabili et corruptibili secundum rationes seminales nisi beneficio luminis corporum super caelestium, quae elongatur a generatione et corruptione, scilicet a sole, lune et stellis";* [21]

and, Jalālu'd Dīn Rūmī: "When the time comes for the embryo to receive the vital spirit, at that time the Sun becomes its helper. This embryo is brought into movement by the Sun, for the Sun is quickly endowing it with spirit. From the other stars this embryo received only an impression, until the Sun shone upon it. By which way did it become connected in the womb with the beauteous Sun? By the hidden way that is remote from our sense-perception." [22]

It would be possible to cite still more material from other sources, for example, from the American Indians, in whose mythologies "virgin" is expressed by "non-sunstruck." But enough has been said to show that there is, or has been, a more or less general agreement that *Spiritus est qui vivificat, caro non prodest quicquam;* [23] and even today there are many who can take seriously the commandment: "Call no *man* your father on earth: for one is your Father, which is in heaven." [24] It is difficult to see how these distinctions of social from spiritual paternity differ essentially from the "official doctrine" of the Australian aborigines.

It seems to me that one cannot claim to have considered their "traditional teachings" in their true perspective if their universality is ignored. In any case, for so long as their beliefs are considered somewhat strange and peculiar, and as the products of an alien type of mentality, the question, How is it that so many and different kinds of men have thought alike? will also be ignored. And is not this a question of the most absorbing interest, and one that is most essentially "anthropological"? If it be true, as Alfred Jeremias said, that the various human cultures are really only the dialects of one and the same spiritual language [25] it is surely proper for the student of man to ask himself when and where this spiritual language may have originated. In any event, how much easier it becomes to understand another people's culture, how much easier to recog-

nize their full humanity, to think with them rather than merely
of or even for them, if the scholar realizes that their "official
doctrines" are the same as those that have long been current
and even now survive in his own environment!

A second example is that of the "puppet complex." Dr.
Margaret Mead makes use of this expression in her account
of Balinese character, where she remarks: "The animated puppet, the doll which dances on a string, the leather puppets
manipulated by the puppeteer, and finally the little girl trance
dancers who themselves become exaggeratedly limp and soft
as they dance to the commands of the audience, all dramatise
this whole picture of involuntary learning, in which it is not
the will of the learner, but the pattern of the situation and the
manipulation of the teacher which prevail"; and speaks of "the
fantasy of the body made of separate independent parts . . . the
notion that the body is like a puppet, just pinned together at
the joints."[26] It is implied that these are especially Balinese
peculiarities. Although the observation is unrelated to any governing first principle, and so not fully understood, it is excellent
in itself: for it is realized that the dancer's puppet-like relaxation
is that of an obedient pupil, who would be guided not by her
own will, but by a teacher's. One cannot but recall the words
of Christ: "I do nothing of myself," and "not what I will, but
what thou wilt."[27] So said Behmen: "Thou shalt do nothing
but forsake thy own will, *viz.* that which thou callest 'I,' or
'thyself.' By which means all thy evil properties will grow
weak, faint, and ready to die; and then thou wilt sink down
again into that one thing, from which thou art originally
sprung."[28] The dancer is not, in fact, expressing "herself," but
altogether an artist, inspired, ἔνθεος: her condition is quite
properly described as one of trance or ecstasy. The whole procedure is a carrying over into art of the vital principle of resignation. Religion and culture, sacred and profane, are undivided.

Actually, this "complex," "fantasy," or "notion"—terms that are employed all too condescendingly—is nothing peculiarly Balinese, but typically both Indian and Platonic, and almost as certainly of Indian origin in Bali as it is of Platonic-Aristotelian derivation in Europe. It is, moreover, bound up with and implies two other doctrines, those of Līlā [29] and the Sūtrātman, [30] and with the traditional symbolism of the theater. [31] Plato sees in puppets (θαυμάτα) with their automatic, autokinetic motions, a typical example of the wonder (τὸ θαυμάζειν) that is the source or beginning of philosophy: it is "as regards the best in us that we are really God's toys" and ought to dance accordingly, obeying only the control of that one cord by which the puppet is suspended from above and not the contrary and unregulated pulls by which external things drag each one to and fro in accordance with his own likes and dislikes. [32] For as Philo also says, "our five senses," together with the powers of speech and generation, "all these, as in puppet-shows are drawn by cords by their Director |ἡγεμονικός|, [33] now resting, now moving, each in the attitudes and motions appropriate to it." [34] For a puppet to behave as it might like were indeed against nature; the movements that are induced by personal appetites are not free, but uncalculated and irregular. But "Nous is never wrong," [35] and "the Daimon always holds me back from what 'I' want to do, and never eggs me on"; [36] and its truth, unlike that of this man Socrates, is irrefutable. [37]

Dr. Margaret Mead refers to the puppet's joints, and these are indeed to be regarded as the cogwheels of a mechanism of which the pins are axles. [38] But what is more important in the puppet symbolism is the thread on which its parts are strung and without which it would fall down inanimate, as actually happens when one "gives up the ghost" and is "cut off." The "notion that the body is like a puppet" does not depend upon a merely external resemblance but far more upon the relation of the guiding thread or threads that the hand of the puppeteer controls, as reins are held by the driver of a vehicle. "Bear in mind that what pulls the string is that Being hidden within us: *that* makes our speech, *that* is our speech, our life, our Man . . . something more Godlike than the passions that make us literally puppets and naught else." [39]

The analogy is formulated in the *Mahābhārata* thus: "Human gestures are harnessed by another, as with a wooden doll strung on a thread." [40] And so the question is asked—"Do you know that Thread by which, and that Inner Controller by whom this world and the other and all beings are strung together and controlled from within, so that they move like a puppet, performing their respective functions?" [41]—or, to ask the same question in other words, know Him *questi nei cor mortali è permotore?* [42] know Him *questi la terra in se stringe?* [43] Elegant wooden shafts well and newly painted, fastened by threads and pins . . . such is the likeness of these limbs of ours." [44] "Who made this (wooden) doll? Where is its maker? Whence has it arisen? How will it perish?" [45] The answers to all these questions had long since been given: "The Sun is the fastening to which these worlds are linked. . . . He strings these worlds to himself by a thread, the thread of the Gale." [46] So it is that "all this universe is strung on Me, like rows of gems on a thread"; [47] and, "verily, he who knows *that* thread, and the Inner Controller who from within controls this and the other world and all beings, he knows Brahma, he knows the Gods, the Vedas, Being, Self and everything." [48] *This* is the background of the "puppet complex" of the Balinese, apart from which it cannot be said that their "character" has been explained, however carefully it may have been observed. [49]

Puppets seem to move of themselves, but are really activated and controlled from within by the thread from which they are suspended from above, and only move intelligently in obedience to this leash: and it is in this automatism, or appearance of free will and self-motion, that the puppet most of all resembles man. Puppets are "automata," yes; but actually no more than any other machines able to move without a power put into them or continuously transmitted to them by an intelligent principle distinct from any or all of their moving parts.[50] Could they also speak the language of the traditional philosophy they would say, "It is not my self, that of these wooden parts, but another Self, the Self of all puppets, that moves me; and if I seem to move of my own will, this is only true to the extent that I have identified myself and all my being and willing with the Puppeteer's[51] who made and moves me." Man-made automata are imitations of the creations of the mythical craftsmen, δημιουργοί, such as Maya, Hephaistos, Daedalus, Regin; and if one is not to misunderstand their significance, it must always be borne in mind that "automatic," which nowadays implies an involuntary and merely reflex activity, had originally an almost exactly opposite meaning, that of "acting of one's own will" or that of "self-moving."[52] The "automatic doors" of the Janua Coeli,[53] the Symplegades generally, and their "automatic" janitors, will be misinterpreted if it is not realized that it is meant that they are "alive," an animation that is explicitly denoted by the representation of the doors as winged in the iconography of the Sundoor on Babylonian seals.

One may now be in a position to understand the transparent myth of the City of Wooden Automata in the *Katha Sarit Sāgara*.[54] Here the hero, Naravāhanadatta—"Theodore"—reaches a marvelous city (*āścaryam puram*) in which the whole citizenry (*paurajanam*) consists of wooden engines or automata (*kāsthamaya-yantram*) all behaving as if alive (*ceṣṭamānam sajīvavat*[55]) although recognizable as lifeless by their want of speech; and this arouses his wonder (*vismayan* = θαῦμα).[56] He enters the palace, and sees there a comely man (*bhavyam*[57] *puruṣam*) enthroned and surrounded by janissaries and female guards; this man is the only consciousness (*ekakaṁ cetanam*[58]) there, and is the cause of motion in the insensible folk, "even as the Spirit overstands the powers of perception and action"— *indriyāṇām ivātmānam adhiṣṭhātṛtayā sthitam.*[59] In reply to questions, the King explains that he, Rājyadhara—the royal power—is one of the two sons of King Bāhubala—"Armstrong"—and that his brother Prāṇadhara—the pneumatic power—having robbed his father's treasury and dallied with his fortune, both have fled. "Both of us," he says, "are carpenters,[51] expert in the making of artful wooden and other automata—or engines, like those produced by Maya"[60]— *takṣaṇau . . . māyā-praṇīteva darvādi-maya-yantra-vicakṣaṇau.* Rājyadhara continues in saying, "I finally reached this empty city [*śūnyam puram*] and entered the palace." There in the heart of the palace he is fed by invisible hands: and "all these automata [*yantra*] are no mere products of my imagination, for I made them. It is by the will of the Disposer that I, even being a carpenter, have come here, and am enjoying the sport of a king, as a God all alone by myself" (*ihāgatya takṣāpi devaikāki karomy ahaṁ rājño līlāyitam*).[61]

No one at all familiar with the traditional Indian or Greek psychology will doubt that the City of Wooden Automata is macrocosmically the world and microcosmically man—the man whose "person," *puru-ṣa,* is so called because of his being the *cit*-izen in every *pol*-itical "body."[62] The "golden palace" is the "heart" of the "Golden City," the center from which all its operations are directed. To Rājyadhara his retainers, the psychic powers of perception and action, like the subjects of earthly kings, bring all kinds of food by which the Spirit is nourished when it thus comes eating and drinking.[63] That his food of all kinds is thus served by invisible hands, and that he repeoples a Waste Land (*śūnyam puram*), is a reminder that he is effectively the "Rich King" of a "Grail Castle." As the "sole consciousness" in the City of Wooden Automata, Rājyadhara corresponds to the "Only Thinker, your Self, the Inner Controller, Immortal" of the Upaniṣads.[64] The original "robbery" referred to is that of the sources of life, the Indian Rape of Soma and the Greek Promethean theft of fire; it is only by such a "theft" that the world can be quickened, but it necessarily involves the separation or exile of the immanent principles from their transcendent source. Rājyadhara rightly speaks of himself as a God.

If there could be any doubt that these are the real meanings of the story of the Golden City (*hemapura*) or that this would have been obvious to almost any Indian hearer, it can be dissipated not only by a consideration of the parallel wordings of the scriptural passages already cited, but also by a comparison with the *Tripurā Rahasya*,[65] where it is again the question of a "city" and its citizens, and it is told that the Migrant or Procedent (*pracāra*),[66] though single, "multiplies himself, manifests as the city and its citizens and pervades them all, protects and holds them," and that "without him they would all be scattered and lost like pearls without the string of the necklace," [67] and it is perfectly clear that, as the text itself later explains, the Migrant is the Breath or Life—*prāṇa*—and the city the body, of which the parts are strung on Him.

All these formulations, furthermore, clarify the meanings of the term *sūtra-dhāra* as stage manager and carpenter or architect; for these are one and the same *in divinis*, and so far as the puppet play is concerned may be one and the same in human practice. One does not have to suppose with Pischel [68] that the Indian drama originated in a puppet play of unknown antiquity; or, on the other hand, that the *sūtra-dhāra* is a "carpenter" merely because he carries a measuring line. The origins of drama and of architecture are mythical, and both are equally "imitations" of divine prototypes.[69] It is because, whether as the Artist who makes or as the Controller who manages his "toys," as Plato calls them, the All-Maker, Viśvakarmā, is the "Holder of Every Thread" (*viśva-sūtra-dhṛk*),[70] that the human artist and the stage manager are, in the likeness and image of God, equally "Holders of a Thread." [71]

Enough has been said to show that the doctrine of "spiritual paternity" is nothing peculiarly Pacific or Australian, and that the so-called "puppet complex" is nothing peculiarly Balinese; enough also to show that the Australian "official doctrine" is an intellectual formulation rather than a proof of nescience,[72] and that the expression "complex," implying a psychosis, is quite irrelevant to describe what is in fact a metaphysical "theory." Such formulations cannot be properly evaluated or seen in any true perspective as long as they are treated as purely local phenomena to be explained in some evolutionary or psychological way on the sole premise of the environment in which they happen to have been observed; but only if they are related to the whole spiritual-cultural horizon into the pattern of which they naturally fit, and of which they may be only the peripheral "superstitions," in the strictly etymological sense of this excellent but much abused term.[73] The student of "primitive beliefs" and of "folklore" must be, if he is not to betray his vocation, not so much a psychologist in the current sense as he must be an accomplished theologian and metaphysician.

These general considerations are also of the highest importance if anthropology is to amount to anything more than another satisfaction of our curiosity; if, that is to say, it is to subserve the good of mankind by enabling men to understand one another, and even to think *with* one another, rather than merely *of* one another as strangers. For example, Marsilio Ficino, Meister Eckhart, William Law, and Hāfiz are thinking *with* one another when all employ the figure of the "hook" with which the Fisher King angles for his human prey; [74] or the Celt is thinking with the Buddhist when both are agreed that "He who would be chief, let him be your bridge." [75] Even so the Australian is thinking with Christ when in fact, having been initiated, he too calls "no man father on earth." And so, as was previously indicated, there is a real connection, though it may have been prehistoric, between Margaret Mead's observation "limp and soft," Jacob Behmen's "weak, faint and ready to die," and the fact that "all scripture cries aloud for freedom from self." It is because of their acceptance of this point of view that, to the modern mentality to which it is so repugnant, the members of traditional and "unanimous" societies seem not yet to have distinguished themselves from their environment; and the irony of the situation is this, that the modern proletarians, to whom the notions of individuality and self-expression are so important, are themselves of all peoples the least individualized and the most like a herd. [76]

A culture such as the Balinese is so completely molded and pervaded by its inherited "official doctrine" that a "correct" or "orthodox" deportment in any given situation has become a second nature: it is now no longer necessary to remember the rules of the game because the habit of the art of life is now engrained. [77] In "forsaking her own will, *viz*. that which thou callest 'I,' or 'thyself,' " the Balinese dancer in her rapt ecstasy is not a product of any peculiarly Balinese "complex," but of the *Philosophia Perennis*.

Plato says that it is as regards *the best in human beings* that they are most really God's playthings. And this notion, that what is called "their" life is really a divine sporting, in which their part is free and active only to the extent that their wills are merged in his who plays the game, is one of man's deepest insights. As Jalālu'd Dīn Rūmī states, "Who so hath not surrendered will, no will hath he." So says also Angelus Silesius:

> *Dieses Alles ist ein Spiel, das ihr der Gottheit macht;*
> *Sie hat die Kreatur um ihretwillen gedacht.*

Whoever accepts this point of view will feel that he "ought" to act accordingly; and as the expression "walking with God," Plato's θεῷ ξυνοπαδεῖν, Skr. *brahmacarya,* implies, this is for the puppet his true Way. The only alternative is that of a *passive* subjection to the "pullings and haulings" of the "ruling passions," rightly so called when they become the determinants of conduct.[78] "Ought" is expressed in Greek by δεῖ, from δέω, "bind," the root in δεσμός, that is, the "bond" by which, as Plutarch says, Apollo binds (συνδεῖ) all things to himself and orders them.[79] That bond is precisely Plato's "golden cord" by which the puppet should be guided if it is to play its proper part, avoiding the disorderly movements that are provoked by its own desires; and the "rein" by which the sensitive steeds must be controlled if they are not to miss the way. This is the "clew" to which one must hold fast, if one is to play the game intelligently, and spontaneously, or "automatically."

In the *Tripurā Rahasya*[80] the picture is drawn of an ideal city-state, that of a characteristically Indian Utopia and at the same time very like Plato's Republic. The Prince, instructed by his wife, has become a free man (*jīvan-mukta*) liberated in this life, here and now from all the "knots of the heart" and above all from the strongest of these, that of the "identification of the flesh with the Self, which identification in its turn gives rise to the incessant flux of happiness and misery," and being liberated, he performs his royal duties efficiently but absentmindedly and "like an actor on the stage" (*naṭavad raṅga-maṇḍale*). Following his example and instruction, all the citizens attain a like liberty, and are no longer motivated by their passions, although still possessing them. The consequences are by no means "antisocial"; on the contrary, wordly affairs are still carried on in this ideal free state, in which its citizens continue to play their parts, by force of former preoccupation, but now "without thinking of past good or evil fortune, or counting on future joys or pains; [81] in their everyday life laughing, rejoicing, wearied or angered, like men intoxicated and indifferent to their own affairs.[82] Wherefore Sanaka and other sages who visited there called it the 'City of Resplendent Wisdom.' "

That in this ideal City of God it is the actor that represents the norm of conduct is especially pertinent in the present context. Here, "all the world's a stage," without distinction of action as conduct from action as drama, and everyone still plays the part that he "ought" to play, if the city is to prosper.[83] The true actor, then, whether in life or in his own profession, "acts without acting" in the sense of the *Bhagavad Gītā* and the Taoist *wei wu wei* doctrine. He does not identify himself with the part, and is not infected (*na lipyate*) by what he does on the stage: his role, as men regard it, may be that of either saint or sinner, but like God he remains himself and untroubled by the thought, "Thus I did right," or "Thus I did wrong,"[84] being above the battle.[85]

So the Balinese dancer, who is not "expressing herself," but playing her part impersonally, is by no means the victim of a "complex," but merely a perfect actress: and the members of any other society, all of whom have their part to play but for the most part want to be "stars," might learn from her, if they would, what is the distinction of acting from merely behaving, which is that of spontaneity from license. It is not enough to have "observed," however accurately: it is only when the anthropologist has profoundly understood what he sees, when he has really entertained the ideas of which the spectacle is a demonstration, that it can become for him a serious experience.[86]

REFERENCES

[1] Montagu, M. F. Ashley, "Nescience, Science and Psycho-Analysis," *Psychiatry* (1941) 4.45-60. References to the literature will be found in this article.

[2] The italics here are original. Those in the two following quotations are mine.

[3] *Majjhima Nikāya* I:265-266. Gandharvas and Apsarases are the rulers with respect to progeny or lack of progeny—*Pañcaviṁśa Brāhmaṇa* IX:3.1.

[4] Philo Judaeus, *Quis rerum divinarum heres* 115.

[5] Plato, *Laws* 773 E.

[6] Ephesians 3:15.

[7] In all these contexts in which "Sun" has been capitalized the reference is, of course, to the "inward Sun" as distinguished from "the outward sun, which receives its power and lustre from the inward"—Behmen, Jacob, *Signatura rerum* XI:75, to the "Sun of the Angels" as distinguished from the "sun of sense"—Dante, *Paradiso* X:53-54; compare *Convito* III:12, 50-60. This "Sun of the sun" —Philo Judaeus, *De specialis legibus* I:279; compare *De cherubim* 97—Apollo as distinguished from Helios—Plato, *Laws* 898 D, Plutarch, *Moralia* 393 D, 400 C, D—is not "the sun whom all men see" but "the Sun whom not all know with the mind"—*Atharva Veda* X:8.14, "whose body the sun is"—*Bṛhadāraṇyaka Upaniṣad* III:7.9. The traditional distinction of intelligible from sensible, invisible from visible "suns" is essential to any adequate understanding of "solar mythologies" and "solar cults."

[8] Aristotle, *Physics* II:2.

[9] Dante, *Paradiso* XXII:116 and XXIX:15.

[10] *Śatapatha Brāhmaṇa* VII:3.2.12. See Coomaraswamy, Ananda K., "Sunkiss," *JAOS* (1940) 60:46-67; and "Primitive Mentality," *Quarterly Journal of the Mythological Society* (1940) 31:69-91. To the Sunkiss corresponds "the caress of Zeus by his on-breathing"— Æschylus, *Suppliants*; 344-345—P. W. Smyth's version.

[11] *Jaiminīya Upaniṣad Brāhmaṇa* III:10.4. Compare *Pañcaviṃśa Brāhmaṇa* XVI:14.5.

[12] *Ṛgveda* VII:102.2. One hardly needs to say or seek to demonstrate that the Christian and pagan solar symbolisms are homologous. An illustration can be cited, however, in St. Ambrose's *Hymnus Matutinus:*

> *Verusque sol, illabere*
> *Micans nitore perpeti;*
> *Jubarque Sancti Spiritūs*
> *Infunde nostris sensibus*

which is an almost literal equivalent of the Vedic Gāyatrī, *Ṛgveda* III:62.10.

[13] *Bṛhadāraṇyaka Upaniṣad* III:9.28.

[14] Reference footnote 13; III:7.23.

[15] This equation is explicit in *Aitareya Āraṇyaka* III:2.3, where also Keith remarks that this is "the most common doctrine in the Upaniṣads." The "Sun" in question is the Sun of *Ṛgveda* I:115.1, "the Spiritual-Self [*ātman*] of all that is noble or immobile."

[16] *Kauṣītaki Upaniṣad* III:3.

[17] *Taittirīya Saṃhitā* VII:1.1.1, *Śatapatha Brāhmaṇa* VIII:7.1.16. Cf. John 1:4 "the life was the light." From the same point of view: *Prima substantiarum est lux . . . Unumquodque quantum habet de luce tantum retinet esse divini*—Witelo, *Liber de intelligentiis* VI, VIII.

[18] *Summa Theologica* III:32.11.

[19] Reference footnote 18; I:45.5.

[20] von Schiller, Johann C., *Wallenstein* III:13.

[21] St. Bonaventura, *De reductione artium ad theologiam* 21; cf. Philo Judaeus, *Quis rerum divinarum heres* 115, "Are not the parents, as it were, concomitant causes only, while [the divine] Nature is the highest, elder and true cause of the begetting of children?" I add "the divine," only to remind the reader that Philo's "Nature" is not the visible and objective world, but that aspect of God's power by which he creates, Plato's αἰειγενὴς φύσις, "the eternal Nature" that we acknowledge in the begetting of descendants—*Laws* 773 E.

It comes to the same thing to say that "the Breath is the progenitive power" and so that "man is propagated from the Breath"—*Pañcaviṃśa Brāhmana* XVI:14.5, since the Breath—*prāṇaḥ*—is commonly identified with the Sun, the pneumatic with the luminous principle.

[22] Jalālu'd Dīn Rūmī, *Mathnawī* I:3775-3779.

[23] John 6:63.

[24] Matthew 23:9.

[25] Jeremias, Alfred, *Handbuch der Altorientalischen Geisteskultur* [2nd ed.]; Berlin, Walter de Gruyter, 1929 (xvii and 508 pp.); in particular, the Foreword.

[26] Bateson, Gregory, and Mead, Margaret, *Balinese Character: A Photographic Analysis,* New York, New York Academy of Sciences, 1942 (xvi and 277 pp.), pp. 17 and 91.

[27] John 8:28; Mark 14:36.

[28] Behmen, Jacob, "Discourse Between Two Souls," *Signatura rerum,* New York, Dutton, n. d. (288 pp.).

[29] Coomaraswamy, Ananda K., "Līlā," *JAOS* (1941) 61:98-101; and "Play and Seriousness," *Journal of Philosophy* (1942) 39:550-552.

[30] Coomaraswamy, Ananda K., "Primitive Mentality," reference footnote 10, p. 82; "Symbolism," *Dictionary of World Literature;* "The Iconography of Dürer's 'Knots' and Leonardo's 'Concatenation,'" *Art Quarterly* (1944) 7:109-128. See also Śaṅkarācārya, *Śataślokī* 12 and 55: man is a bead strung on the thread of the conscious Self, and just as wooden puppets are worked by strings, so the world is operated by the Thread-Spirit.

[31] Cf. Guénon, René, *"Le symbolisme du théâtre,"* Le Voile d'Isis (1932) 37:65-70.

[32] Plato, *Theatetus* 155 D; and *Laws* 644 and 803-844.

[33] *Dux,* Duke, Leader, Guide; the solar Leader; netṛ of Ṛgveda V:50.1 and "Self of self, the Immortal Leader"—ātmano' tmā netāmṛtaḥ, of *Maitri Upaniṣad* VI:7.

[34] Philo Judaeus, *De opificio mundi* 117.

[35] Aristotle, *De anima* III:10, 433 A.

[36] Plato, *Apology* 31 D; and *Phaedrus* 242 B.

[37] Plato, *Symposium* 201 C.

[38] It is not so much the function of the pins to hold the joints together as to enable the limbs to move freely. Pegs (γόμφοι, Plato, *Timaeus* 43 A)—on which the joints (ἄρθρα) move, and comparable to the hinges (γόμφοι) of doors (Parmenides in Sextus Empiricus, *Adversus dogmatos* 111)—are, indeed, employed; and these are also called pivots (στρόφιγγες), but the limbs are bound together by the

sinews (νεῦρα) that tighten and loosen round the pivots, and so move the parts of the body as if on hinges—*Timaeus* 74 B. These sinews are the physical counterparts of the psychic "bonds of life"—*Timaeus* 73 B—that are dissolved at death—*Timaeus* 81 E; Philo Judaeus, *Quis rerum divinarum heres* 242, *Bṛhadāraṇyaka Upaniṣad* II:7.2; *Maitri Upaniṣad* 1:4. It is by the "thread" that the parts are really co-ordinated and moved: as in man "it is by the Breath that the joints are united," *prāṇena sarvāṇi parvāṇi saṃdadhāti,* the vital Breath that is called the "Thread-Spirit," *sūtrātman,* "that links up [*saṃtanoti*] this world"—*Aitareya Āraṇyaka* I:4.2,3. See other references in reference footnote 30.

[39] Marcus Aurelius, X:38 and XII:19; cf. II:2, III:16, VI:16, VII:3, VII:29.

The puppet symbolism is closely related to the Indian, Platonic, Neoplatonic, and later symbolism of the chariot, of which the steeds are the sensitive powers that seek their own pastures and must be curbed and guided by the knowing driver, the Reason, who only knows the Way or "Royal Road."

[40] *Mahābhārata,* Udyoga Parvan 32:12.

[41] *Bṛhadāraṇyaka Upaniṣad* III:7.1; cf. 4.1, combined with Śankara's commentaries.

[42] Dante, *Paradiso* I:116: corresponding to *Maitri Upaniṣad* II:6, "from within this heart of ours, the Mover," *asmād-dhṛd-antarāt pracodayitṛ.*

[43] Dante, reference footnote 42, I:117.

[44] *Therīgāthā* 390, 391.

[45] *Saṃyutta Nikāya* I:134.

[46] *Śatapatha Brāhmaṇa* VI:7.1.17 and VIII:7.3.10.

[47] *Bhagavad Gītā* VII:7; compare *Tripurā Rahasya,* Jñāna Khaṇḍa, V:119-124—reference footnote 65.

[48] *Bṛhadāraṇyaka Upaniṣad* III:7.1.

[49] The reviewer of another work of Dr. Margaret Mead's, *The American Character,* one of the Pelican Books, justly remarks on "the danger of . . . providing psychological, or even biological reasons for traits which should be treated metaphysically"—*New English Weekly* (1944) 25:132. The "psychological" explanations themselves will be inadequate if the traditional psychology, for example, that of Philo and the *Bhagavad Gītā,* is overlooked. In this traditional psychology it is maintained that there can be no greater error or source

of evil than to conceive that *"I* am the doer." From the point of view of anyone who accepts this axiology, the behavior of the Balinese dancer is simply *natural,* and that of the modern, self-expressive "artist," *unnatural.*

[50] For example, when La Mettrie says, "The human body is a machine that winds its own springs," he is "explaining" a phenomenon by something else of a sort that never was on sea or land, something as inconceivable as "the son of a barren woman." When he continues by saying that "the soul is but a principle of motion or material and sensible part of the brain," he is propounding two entirely different theories, of which the first is Plato's, and the second reverts to his own unthinkable "machine." My citation of La Mettrie is taken from Urban, Wilbur Marshall, *Language and Reality,* New York, Macmillan, 1939 (755 pp.); in particular p. 314.

In what sense man can be properly compared to a machine is discussed by Schrödinger, Erwin, *What is Life?,* Cambridge, Macmillan, 1945.

[51] Skr. *sūtra-dhāra,* "holder of the thread," and so "puppeteer," "stage manager," and "carpenter." It is not insignificant, also, that the puppets are "wooden"; the "primary matter" of which the world is made being a "wood"—ΰλη, Skr. *vana*—and the maker therefore a "carpenter."

[52] *Iliad* II:408; Hesiod, *Marriage of Ceyz* 2 and *Opus* 103, where the term is used of persons or personified powers. Aristotle, *Physics* II:6, indeed, interprets "automaton" to mean "in itself to no purpose," and so "accidental" or "random"; but this is inconsistent with the meanings already cited and with the use of αὐτόματον with φύω, "grow"—cf. Skr. *svaruḥ*—and according to most scholars the root meaning is that of "acting of one's own will." The true analogy is with τὸ ἑαυτὸ χινεῖν, "self-motion," which is the highest kind of motion—Plato, *Phaedrus* 264 A, *Laws* 895. The problem turns, as usual, upon the question, What or which is the "self" implied, outer mortal or inner immortal?—the latter being the true ἡγεμονιχός.

[53] *Iliad* V:409; compare *Suparṇādhyāya* XXV:1, and the "Active Doors" of Celtic mythology.

[54] *Kathā Sarit Sāgara* VII:9.1-59—tar. 43, see Penzer, N. M., *Ocean of the Streams of Story* (1925) 3: begin p. 280, and further 3:56 and 9:149; Penzer discusses automata, but he has not the least conception of their theory.

[55] *Ceṣṭamānam* corresponding to *ceṣṭate* in the *Mahābhārata*, reference footnote 40.

[56] Such "wonder" as is the beginning of philosophy, Plato, *Theatetus* 155 D, and Aristotle, *Metaphysics* 982 B.

[57] *Bhavya*, future participle of *bhū*, "become," takes on the sense of "comely" in the same way that English "becoming" takes on the meaning "suitable," "as it should be."

[58] The formulas here are very closely related to those of *Maitri Upaniṣad* II:6 and *Bhagavad Gītā* XVIII:61. In the *Upaniṣad*, Prajāpati, "from within the heart," animates and motivates his otherwise lifeless offspring, setting them up in possession of consciousness (*cetanavat*). In the Gītā Śrī Krishna, speaking of himself, says: "The Lord, seated in the heart of all beings, maketh them all, by his art, to wander about, mounted on their engines," *īśvaraḥ sarvabhūtānāṁ hṛddeśe . . . tiṣṭhati, bhrāmayan sarvabhūtāni yantrārūḍhāni māyayā.*

[59] This is, again, a statement of the traditional psychology that everywhere underlies the "puppet complex" and the chariot symbolism; cf. reference footnote 49.

[60] The Titan Maya, who may be compared to Hephaistos, Daedalus, Wayland, and Regin, is the great Artist whose daughter, in the *Kathā Sarit Sāgara* VI:3, Penzer 3:42, Somaprabhā, exhibits a variety of engines or automata, and explains that these artful and self-empowered wooden dolls, these crafty mechanical works of art (*kāṣṭhamayīh sva-māyā-yantra-putrikāh . . . māyā-yantrādi-śilpāni*) were originally "emanated [*sṛṣṭāni*] by my father of old," and that there are five sorts corresponding, like "that great engine, the world" (cf. Marsilio Ficino, *Symposium* IV.5, *"machino del mondo"*), to the five elements, "but the Wheel that guards the Water of Life, that he alone, and no other, understands."

[61] On this royal "sport" see reference footnote 29, and cf. also Clement of Alexandria, *Instructor* I; chapter 5: "O wise sport, laughter assisted by endurance, and the king as spectator . . . and this is the divine sport. 'Such a sport of his own, Jove sports,' says Heracleitus. The King, then, who is Christ, beholds from above our laughter, and looking through the window, views the thanksgiving and the blessing." Clement's "spectator" corresponds to the *prekṣaka* of *Maitri Upaniṣad* II:7.

"But the Nitya and the Līlā are the two aspects of the same reality. . . . The Absolute plays in many ways: as Īśvara, as the gods, as man, and as the universe. The Incarnation is the play of the Absolute as man . . . The formless God is real, and equally real is God with form."—*The Gospel of Srī Rāmakrishna*, New York, Rāmakrishna-Vivekananda Center, 1942 (xxiii and 1063 pp.), pp. 358-359.

62 This assumes the etymology of *puruṣa* as given in *Bṛhadāra-ṇyaka Upaniṣad* II:5.18, and the connection of *ṣī* with κεῖσθαι. I have dealt more fully with the Indian and corresponding Greek concept of man as a City of God—*brahmapura, Hieropolis, Civitas Dei*—in my "Civilization" in the *Albert Schweitzer Jubilee Volume* (ed. A. Roback, Cambridge, 1946).

63 "That Golden Person in the Sun, who from his golden place looks down upon this earth, is even He who dwells in the lotus of the heart, and eateth there of food," *Maitri Upaniṣad* V:1; cf. *Ṛgveda* X:90.2, "When He rises up by food." "He, indeed, is the great, unborn Spiritual-Self, who is the Discriminant amongst the powers of the soul. In the ether of the heart reclines the Ruler of All, the Lord of All, the King of All," *Bṛhadāraṇyaka Upaniṣad* IV:4.22; cf. *Chāndogya Upaniṣad* VIII:1.1-6. "To this same Life [*prāṇa*] as Brahma, all these divinities bring tribute unasked," *Kauṣītaki Upaniṣad* II:1, cf. *Atharva Veda* X:7.39 and 8.15. In all these contexts, as for Plato, "food" is whatever aliment nourishes the physical or psychic powers, body or mind.

64 *Bṛhadāraṇyaka Upaniṣad* III:8.23; "He who sets up this body in possession of consciousness, and moves it," *Maitri Upaniṣad* 11.6.

65 Jñāna Khanda V:119-124—Iyer, M. S. Venkatarama [tr.], Jñāna Khanda. *Quart. J. Myth. Soc.* (1937) 28:170-219, 269-289; (1938) 29:39-57, 189-207; (1939) 29:329-351, 466-499—the text in the *Sarasvati Bhavana Texts, Number 15* (1925-1933).

66 In theology, "procession" is the coming forth or manifestation of the deity as or in a Person. This appearance on the stage of the world is a "descent"—*avataraṇa*—strictly comparable to that of the actor who emerges from the greenroom to appear in some disguise. The reference of the text is to the procession of the Spirit, *prajñātman* or *prāṇa*.

67 As in the *Bhagavad Gītā* VII:7. Cf. reference footnote 30.

68 Pischel, Richard, *Die Heimat des Puppenspiels*, Halle, Hallesche Rektorreden II, 1900; for the English version refer to Tawney, Mil-

dred C., *The Home of the Puppet Play*, London, Luzac, 1902 (32 pp.).

⁶⁹ "Human works of art are imitations of divine prototypes." *Aitareya Brāhmaṇa* VI:27.

⁷⁰ This term occurs with reference to Vishnu as the Creator.

⁷¹ It has been well said by the late Professor Arthur Berriedale Keith that "it is indeed to ignore how essentially religion enters into the life of the Hindu to imagine that it is possible to trace the beginnings of drama to a detached love of amusement."—*The Sanskrit Drama*, Oxford, Clarendon Press, 1924 (405 pp.), p. 52. In dealing with any traditional civilization it must always be realized that no real distinction can be drawn there as of culture from religion or profane from sacred. Such distinctions, like that of utility or *value* from meaning or *beauty*, are the products of a modern schizophrenia.

⁷² A blind faith in "progress" makes it all too easy to accuse the "backward races" of ignorance or a "prelogical mentality." "*Lorsque nous ne comprenons pas un phénomène iconographique, nous sommes toujours tentés de dire que nous comprenons fort bien—mais que c'est indigène qui est maladroit ou n'a pas compris*," Hentze, Carl, *Objets rituels, croyances et dieux de la Chine antique et de l'Amérique*, Anvers, "De Sikkel" Editions, 1936 (119 pp., 230 figs., 12 plates); in particular p. 33. "*Das Märchenhaft-Wunderbare muss daher mit ganz anderen Augen als mit unseren naturwissenschaftlich geschulten angesehen werden*," Preuss, K. Th., in Thurnwald, R., *Lehrbuch der Völkerkunde* (1939), p. 127.

⁷³ "Backward communities are the oral libraries of the world's ancient cultures" (Chadwick, N. K., *Poetry and Prophecy*, Cambridge University Press, 1942 [xvi and 110 pp.], xv). "These beliefs of theirs have been preserved until now as a relic of former knowledge" (Aristotle, *Metaphysics* XII:8.10). "*La mémoire collective conserve quelquefois certains détails précis d'une 'théorie' devenue depuis longtemps inintelligible . . . des symboles archaïques d'essence purement métaphysique*"—Eliade, Mircea, *Les livres populaires dans la littérature roumaine*," *Zalmoxis* (1939) II:78. If the fundamental sources of custom and belief are those of a metaphysical tradition, the anthropologist in search of explanation and understanding must be familiar with this tradition.

⁷⁴ Marsilio Ficino, ". . . . the soul inflamed by the divine splendor . . . is secretly lifted up by it as if by a hook in order to become God."

Opera Omnia, p. 306, cited by Kristeller, P. O., *The Philosophy of Marsilio Ficino,* New York, Columbia University Press, 1943 (xiv and 441 pp.)—half title: "Columbia Studies in Philosophy," Number 6; p. 267. "For love is like the fisherman's hook"—Pfeiffer, Franz, *Meister Eckhart,* Göttingen, Vandenhoek and Ruprecht, 1924 (x and 686 pp.), p. 29. "Love is my bait . . . it will put its hook into your heart," William Law, cited by Stephen Hobhouse, *William Law,* 1943, p. 109. Hāfiz, "Fish-like in the sea behold me swimming, till he with his hook my rescue maketh," Leaf, Walter, *Versions from Hafiz* (1898) n:XII. All implied by Mark 1:17, "I will make you fishers of men." There are but few doctrines or symbols that can be adequately studied on the basis of single sources to which they seem to be peculiar if their universality is overlooked.

[75] See Coomaraswamy, Doña Luisa, "The Perilous Bridge of Welfare," *HJAS* (1944) 8:196-213. Cf. the Roman *Imperator,* who was also the *Pontifex Maximus.*

[76] Nothing, of course, is stranger or more unwelcome to the modern mentality than is the idea of "self-naughting." Liberty of choice has become an obsession; the superior liberty of spontaneity is no longer understood. For those who are afraid I cite: "I can no more doubt . . . what to me is fact, perceived truth; namely, that any person would be infinitely happier if he could accept the loss of his 'individual self' and let nature pursue her uncharted course." Hadley, Ernest E., *Psychiatry* (1942) 5:131-134; p. 134. Cf. Sullivan, Harry Stack, *Psychiatry* (1938) 1:121-134. "Here (in the emphasized individuality of each of us, 'myself') we have the very mother of illusions, the ever pregnant source of preconceptions that invalidate all our efforts to understand other peoples. The psychiatrist may, in his more objective moments, hold the correct view of personality, that it is the hypothetical entity that one postulates to account for the doings of people . . . in his less specialized moments the same psychiatrist joins the throng in exploiting his delusions of unique individuality. He conceives himself to be a self-limited unit that alternates between a state of insular detachment and varying degrees of contact with other people and with cultural entities. He arrogates to himself the principal rôle in such of his actions as he 'happens' to notice." To believe in one's own or another's "personality" or "individuality" is animism. In the traditional philosophy it is emphasized that "personalities" are inconstants, ever changing and never stopping to "be";

"we" are not entities, but processes. Dr. Sullivan's words are—whether or not by intention—an admirable summary of the Buddhist doctrine of *anattā*. An attachment of permanent value to personality will be impossible for anyone who has seen things "as become"—*yathā-bhūtam,* objectively, as causally determined processes. The first step on the way to a liberation from "the mother of illusions," and so toward an "infinite happiness," is to have realized by a demonstration that "this (body and mind) is not my Self," that there is no such thing as a "personality" anywhere to be found in the world. Life in a world of time and space is a condition of incessant change; and, as Plato asks, "How can that which is never in the same state *be* anything?"—*Cratylus* 439 E. Almost the first step in clear thinking is to distinguish *becoming* from *being*. The important thing is to know what "we" really *are;* but this is a knowledge that can only be acquired to the extent that "we" eliminate from our consciousness of being, all that "we" are not. This is the Platonic κάθαρσις, Skr. *śuddha karaṇa.*

[77] Contemporary western dancing is hardly more than a kind of calisthenics, and a spectacle; in the traditional art, which survives elsewhere, "all the dancer's gestures are signs of things, and the dance is called rational, because it aptly signifies and displays something over and above the pleasure of the senses."—St. Augustine, *De ordine* 34: cf. Coomaraswamy, Ananda K., and Duggirala, G. K., *Mirror of Gesture,* New York, Weyhe, 1936 (81 pp. and 20 plates). "Physical exercise, the type of the former, while it may induce a certain kinesthetic enjoyment, does not, in its net effect, go far beyond the muscles, the lungs, the circulatory system, and so on. Play activity, on the other hand, has as a result a restoration of what we may generally term a rational balance [note: Andrae's 'polar balance of physical and metaphysical']. It is true that, in so far as play is recreation, it is escape. It is an escape from the relative chaos of ordinary experience to a world where there is a rational and moral order, plainly visible, and not simply the object of faith. The play is, then, like art, a clarification of experience . . . almost identical with a sense of freedom. The real hindrance to freedom is not rules but chance; the rules of the game make possible the freedom within its framework."—Seward, George, *Journal of Philosophy* (1944) 41:184. It is just this "clarification" that the anthropologist misses, when he merely "observes" with scientific "objectivity" and "detachment," hardly to be

distinguished from condescension. "This, in fact, is the Western way of hiding one's own heart under the cloak of so-called scientific understanding. We do it partly because of the *misérable vanité des savants* which fears and rejects with horror any sign of living sympathy, and partly because an understanding that reaches the feelings might allow contact with the foreign spirit to become a serious experience."—Jung, C. G., and Wilhelm, Richard, *Secret of the Golden Flower,* London, Kegan, Paul, 1932 (ix and 151 pp., 10 plates); in particular p. 77. I say that anthropology is useless, or almost useless, if it does not lead to any such experience.

It hardly needs to be said that I am not accusing either of the two authors cited of "vanity" or want of "living sympathy." Professor Ashley Montagu, for example, has said that "in spite of our emormous technological advances we are spiritually, and as humane beings, not the equals of the average Australian aboriginal or the average Eskimo —we are very definitely their inferiors." Montagu, M. F. Ashley, "Socio-Biology of Man," *Sci. Monthly* (1940) 50:483-490. It is to such writers as Sir J. G. Frazer and Lévy-Bruhl that Jung's critique really applies.

[78] On this passive subjection compare *Chāndogya Upaniṣad* VIII: 1.5 and Philo Judaeus, *Quis rerum divinarum heres,* 186. The distinction involved is that of will from desire: "the spirit is willing, but the flesh is weak." To do as one "likes" is the antithesis of free will; the free man much rather likes what he does than does what he likes.

[79] Plutarch, *Moralia,* 393 *f.,* and cf. references in footnote 30.

[80] Jñāna Khaṇḍa X:43-62; reference footnote 65.

[81] In other words, "letting their dead bury their dead," and "taking no thought for the morrow"; living as nearly as possible in the eternal now.

[82] The method in their madness being that they still lived naturally, placing no forcible restraints on their feelings and so, as another translator adds, "dissipating their latent tendencies." One may recall Blake's saying, "Desires suppressed breed pestilence."

[83] The persons mentioned include the princes, men, women, young and old, actors, singers, fools, professors, ministers, artisans, and hetaerae.

[84] *Bṛhadāraṇyaka Upaniṣad* IV:4.22.

[85] It is expressly said that the Prince regarded gain and loss, friend

and foe, impartially: as in the *Bhagavad Gītā* the principle is enunciated, "Thy concern is with the action only, not with the result." One remembers, with Walt Whitman, that "battles are lost in the same spirit in which they are won"; and that the soldier's vocation does not require him to hate, but only to fight well. This last is admirably illustrated by the well-known story of 'Ali who, engaged in single combat, was on the point of victory, but when his opponent spat in his face, withdrew, because he would not fight in anger.

[86] On the distinction of understanding from psychological analysis, see Urban, Wilbur Marshall, *The Intelligible World,* London, Allen and Unwin, and New York, Macmillan, 1929 (479 pp.), pp. 184, 185. Understanding requires a recognition of common values. For so long as men cannot think *with* other peoples they have not understood, but only known them; and in this situation it is largely an ignorance of their own intellectual heritage that stands in the way of understanding and makes an unfamiliar way of thinking seem to be "queer." It lies peculiarly within the province of anthropology to enable men to *understand* one another.

Chapter VII

GRADATION, EVOLUTION, AND REINCARNATION

THE so-called conflicts of religion and science are, for the most part, the result of a mutual misunderstanding of their respective terms and range. As to range: one deals with the why of things, the other with their how; one with intangibles, the other with things that can be measured, whether directly or indirectly. The question of terms is important. At first sight the notion of a creation completed "in the beginning" seems to conflict with the observed origin of species in temporal succession. But ἐν ἀρχῇ, *in principio, agre* do not mean only "in the beginning" with respect to a period of time, but also "in principle," that is, in an ultimate source logically rather than temporally prior to all secondary causes, and no more before than after the supposed beginning of their operation. So, as Dante says, "Neither before nor after was God's moving on the face of the waters"; and Philo, "At that time, indeed, all things took place simultaneously . . . but a sequence was necessarily written into the narrative because of their subsequent generation from one another"; and Behmen, "It was an everlasting beginning."

As Aristotle says, "Eternal beings are not in time." God's existence is, therefore, *now*—the eternal now that separates past from future durations but is not itself a duration, however short. Therefore, in Meister Eckhart's words, "God is creating the whole world *now,* this instant." Again, no sooner has some time elapsed, however little, but everything is changed; πάντα ῥεῖ, "You cannot dip your feet twice in the same waters." So, then, as for Jalālu'd Dīn Rūmī, "Every instant thou art dying, and returning; Muhammad hath said that this world is but a moment. . . . Every moment the world is renewed, life is ever arriving anew, like the stream. . . . The beginning, which is thought, eventuates in action; know that in such wise was the construction of the world in eternity."

In all this there is nothing to which the natural scientist can object; he may, indeed, reply that his interest is confined to the operation of mediate causes, and that it does not extend to questions of a first cause or of the whatness of life; but that is simply a definition of his self-chosen field. The Ego is the only content of the Self that can be known objectively, and therefore the only one that he is willing to consider. His concern is only with behavior.

Empirical observation is always of things that change, that is, of individual things or classes of individual things; of which, as all philosophers are agreed, it cannot be said that they *are,* but only that they become or evolve. The physiologist, for example, investigates the body, and the psychologist the soul or individuality. The latter is perfectly aware that the continued being of individualities is only a postulate, convenient and even necessary for practical purposes, but intellectually untenable; and in this respect he is in complete agreement with the Buddhist, who is never tired of insisting that body and soul—composite and changeable, and therefore wholly mortal—"are not my Self," not the Reality that must be known if we are to "become what we are." In the same way St. Augustine points out that those who saw that both of these, body and soul, are mutable, have sought for what is immutable, and so found God— that One, of which or whom the Upanishads declare that "that art thou." Theology, accordingly, coinciding with autology, prescinds from all that is emotional, to consider only that which does *not* move—"Change and decay in all around I see, O Thou who changest not." It finds him in that eternal *now* that always separates the past from the future and without which these paired terms would have no meaning whatever, just as space would have no meaning were it not for the point that distinguishes here from there. Moment without duration, point without extension—these are the Golden Mean, and inconceivably Strait Way leading out of time into eternity, from death to immortality.

Our experience of "life" is evolutionary: *what* evolves? Evolution is reincarnation, the death of one and the rebirth of another in momentary continuity: *who* reincarnates? Metaphysics prescinds from the animistic proposition of Descartes, *Cogito ergo sum*, to say, *Cogito ergo EST*; and to the question, *Quid est?* answers that this is an improper question, because its subject is not a what amongst others but the whatness of them all and of all that they are not. Reincarnation—as currently understood to mean the return of individual souls to other bodies here on earth—is not an orthodox Indian doctrine, but only a popular belief. So, for example, as Dr. B. C. Law remarks, "It goes without saying that the Buddhist thinker repudiates the notion of the passing of an ego from one embodiment to another." We take our stand with Śrī Śaṅkarācārya when he says, "In truth, there is no other transmigrant but the Lord"—he who is both transcendently himself and the immanent Self in all beings, but never himself becomes anyone; for which there could be cited abundant authority from the Vedas and Upanishads. If, then, we find Śrī Krishna saying to Arjuna, and the Buddha to his Mendicants, "Long is the road that we have trodden, and many are the births that you and I have known," the reference is not to plurality of essences, but to the Common Man in everyman, who in most men has forgotten himself, but in the reawakened has reached the end of the road, and having done with all becoming, is no longer a personality in time, no longer anyone, no longer one of whom one can speak by a proper name.

The Lord is the only transmigrant. That art thou—the very Man in everyman. So, as Blake says:

"Man looks out in tree, herb, fish, beast, collecting up the scattered portions of his immortal body . . .

Wherever a grass grows or a leaf buds, the Eternal Man is seen, is heard, is felt,

And all his sorrows, till he reassumes his ancient bliss";

Māṇikka Vāçagar:

"Grass, shrub was I, worm, tree, full many a sort of beast, bird, snake, stone, man and demon . . .

In every species born, Great Lord! this day I've gained release";

Ovid:

"The spirit wanders, comes now here, now there, and occupies whatever frame it pleases. From beasts it passes into human bodies, and from our bodies into beasts, but never perishes."

Taliesin:

"I was in many a guise before I was disenchanted, I was the hero in trouble, I am old and I am young";

Empedocles:

"Before now I was born a youth and a maiden, a bush and a bird, and a dumb fish leaping out of the sea";

Jalālu'd Dīn Rūmī:

"First came he from the realm of the inorganic, long years dwelt he in the vegetable state, passed into the animal condition, thence towards humanity: whence, again, there is another migration to be made";

Aitareya Āraṇyaka:

"He who knows the Self more and more clearly is more and more fully manifested. In whatever plants and trees and animals there are, he knows the Self more and more fully manifested. For in plants and trees only the plasm

is seen, but in animals intelligence. In them the Self becomes more and more evident. In man the Self is yet more
and more evident; for he is most endowed with providence,
he says what he has known, he sees what he has known,
he knows the morrow, he knows what is and is not mun-
dane, and by the mortal seeks the immortal. But as for the
others, animals, hunger and thirst are the degree of their
discrimination."
In sum, in the words of Farīdu'd Dīn 'Aṭṭār:

"Pilgrim, Pilgrimage, and Road was but Myself
toward Myself."

This is the traditional doctrine, not of "reincarnation" in the
popular and animistic sense, but of the transmigration and evolution of "the ever-productive Nature"; it is one that in no way
conflicts with or excludes the actuality of the process of evolution
as envisaged by the modern naturalist. On the contrary, it is
precisely the conclusion to which, for example, Erwin Schrödinger is led by his enquiry into the facts of heredity in his book
entitled *What is Life?* In his concluding chapter on "Deter-
minism and Freewill," his "only possible inference" is that "I
in the widest meaning of the word—that is to say every conscious mind that has ever said or felt 'I'—am the person, if any,
who controls 'the motion of the atoms' according to the Laws
of Nature. . . . Consciousness is a singular of which the
plural is unknown."

Schrödinger is perfectly aware that this is the position enunciated in the Upanishads, and most succinctly in the formulas,
"That art thou . . . other than Whom there is no other seer,
hearer, thinker or agent."

I cite him here not because I hold that the truth of traditional
doctrines can be proved by laboratory methods, but because his

position so well illustrates the main point I am making, namely that there are no necessary conflicts of science with religion, but only the possibility of a confusion of their respective fields; and the fact that for the whole man, in whom the integration of the Ego with the Self has been effected, there is no impassable barrier between the fields of science and religion. Natural scientist and metaphysician—one and the same man can be both; there need be no betrayal of either scientific objectivity on the one hand or of principles on the other.[2]

REFERENCES

[1] Reprinted from *Main Currents in Modern Thought*, Summer 1946, and *Blackfriars*, November 1946. In *Blackfriars* the following introduction by Bernard Kelly preceded the article:

The following essay by Dr. Coomaraswamy is offered to *Blackfriars* readers for the very high degree of interest which attaches to the approach from an unfamiliar standpoint to the familiar problem of the relation of science to religion.

The metaphysical focus of the essay may perhaps be best obtained from the brilliant paragraph on the *Cogito* of Descartes. Here the startling character of the thought is due to the contrast of the respective ways in which the imagination of East and West lends support to the concept of being. If the West, especially in that caricature of itself which is called modern philosophy, has tended to imagine reality in terms of visible solids, thus coloring the concept of being with an externality and a rigidity of outline not wholly its own, the imagination of the East has generally been more suggestive of a conception of being as an *act,* personal or impersonal as the point of view changes.

For St. Thomas also, being is an "act" to which, ultimately, even substance among the categories is potential, and, to that extent, relative. From no other position available to the West can fruitful contact be made with the tradition Dr. Coomaraswamy represents.

From a deepened understanding of the principles of St. Thomas's metaphysics, it may be possible, now that Eastern writers are more readily available to explain their own thought to us, to carry the understanding of Eastern tradition further than the position outlined in the *De Unitate Intellectus contra Averrhoistas*. In any case it is certain that the unity, or rather the non-duality, of consciousness of which Dr. Coomaraswamy speaks, has nothing to do with the evolutionary and sentimental conceptions of theological modernism.

BERNARD KELLY

[2] The short essay above summarizes a position outlined in my "On the One and Only Transmigrant" (*AOS. Suppl.* 3, 1944) and to be more fully developed with adequate documentation in a work on reincarnation to be completed shortly. The position assumed is that all the traditional texts, Indian, Islamic, and Greek, that seem to assert a reincarnation of individual essences are expressions in terms of a popular, pragmatic animism—"animistic" in the sense that they assume the reality of the postulated Ego—and should be understood metaphysically as having reference only to the universality of the immanent Spirit, Daimon, or Eternal Man-in-this-man, who realizes his own *ex tempore* omnipresence when he "reassumes his ancient bliss."

Chapter VIII

THE BUGBEAR OF DEMOCRACY,
FREEDOM AND EQUALITY [1]

OF all the forces that stand in the way of a cultural synthesis, or as I would rather say, in the way of a mutual understanding indispensible for co-operation, the greatest are those of ignorance and prejudice. Ignorance and prejudice underlie the naive presumption of a "civilizing mission," which to the "backward" peoples against whom it is directed and whose cultures it proposes to destroy, appears a simple impertinence and a proof of the provincialism of the modern West, which regards all imitation as sincerest flattery, even when it amounts to caricature, at the same time that it is ready to take up arms in self-defence if the imitation becomes so real as to involve a rivalry in the economic sphere. Actually, if there is to be any growth of good will on earth, the white man will have to realize that he must live in a world predominantly coloured (and "coloured" for him usually means "backward," i.e. unlike himself); and the Christian will have to realize that he is living in a world predominantly non-Christian. These things will have to be realized and accepted, without indignation or regret. Before a world government can even be dreamed of, we must have citizens of the world, who can meet their fellow citizens without embarrassment, as gentlemen meet gentlemen, and not as would-be school masters meeting pupils who are to be "compulsorily," even if also "freely" educated. There is no more place in the world for the frog in a well who can judge others only by his own experience and mores. We have got to realize, for example, that as El Glaoui, the Pasha of Marrakesh lately said, "the Moslem world does not want the wondrous American world or the incredible American way of life. We (Moslems) want the world of the Koran," and that, *mutatis mutandis*, the like holds good for the majority of Orientals, a majority that includes not only all those who are still "cultured and illiterate," but also a far larger number of those who have spent years of life and study in the West than might be supposed, for it is among these

---

[1] This previously unpublished essay was found among Coomaraswamy's papers; it forms part of his projected series on modern "bugbears," of which only one other has been published ("The Bugbear of Literacy," in *Am I My Brother's Keeper?*, New York: John Day, 1947). This essay could not have been written earlier than 1944.

that many of the most convinced "reactionaries" are to be found.[1] Sometimes, "the more we see of democracy, the more we value monarchy"; the more we see of "equality," the less we admire "that monster of modern growth, the financial-commercial state" in which the majority lives by its "jobs," and the dignity of a vocation or profession is reserved for the very few, and where, in the words of Eric Gill, "on the one hand we have the artist concerned solely to express himself; on the other is the workman deprived of any self to express."

I have long had in mind to write a series of essays on "bugbears." "Am I My Brother's Keeper?" (which appeared in *Asia and the Americas*, March, 1943) may be regarded as the Preface). "The Bugbear of Literacy" appears in the February 1944 issue of the same journal. Others projected include "The Bugbear of Scholarship," "The Bugbear of Woman's Emancipation" (by my wife), "The Bugbear of World Trade," and "The Bugbear of Spiritual Pride," the last with special reference to the improper use of such pejorative terms as "natural religion" and "idolatry." Perhaps these will never be written, for I, too, have a vocation, which is much rather one of research in the field of the significance of the universal symbols of the Philosophia Perennis than one of apology for or polemic on behalf of doctrines that must be believed if they are to be understood, and must be understood if they are to be believed.

In the present article I propose to discuss the prejudices that are aroused in every hundred per cent progressive and democratic-egalitarian mind by the (Portuguese) word "caste." Dr. Niebuhr,

---

[1] Cf. Demetra Vaka, *Haremlik* (1909), p. 139, where the speaker is a young Turkish woman of high birth, well acquainted with the masters of Western literature. She says: "From what I read in your (American) papers, I do not like your world, and I am glad that I am a Mahometan girl." On another page the author asks a Turkish friend, "Don't you really sometimes wish you were a free European woman." and receives the baffling answer, "I have never seen a European man to whom I should like to belong." Again, p. 259, she is told "When, as a girl, I had read about European life it had seemed to me so attractive, so wonderful. But when I came to taste it, it was empty and bitter." Speaking for herself, Demetra Vaka (p. 221) says: "Among the Orientals I am always overwhelmed by a curious feeling of resigned happiness, such as the West can hardly conceive of."

Because you cannot conceive of it, it angers you to think that men and women can be happy under conditions that would be irksome to you, as you now are, you whose ambition is to be "somebody." You do not understand that there can be a higher ambition, to become a "nobody." Resignation to the will of God, that is the very meaning of Islam; contentment, *cultiver son jardin*; these are *our* ambitions. It is not against *our* pattern of life that we Orientals "protest and rebel," but against your interference. It is *your* way of life that we repudiate, whereever it has not already corrupted us.

for example, calls the Indian caste system "the most rigid form of class snobbishness in history"; he means of course, "class *arrogance*," since he must have intended to criticize the supposed attitude of the higher castes (comparable to that of Englishmen in India, and to that of those who maintain the Mason-Dixon line in America), while it is, by dictionary definition, only an inferior that can be a "snob." But how can there be either arrogance or snobbishness where there is no social ambition? It is in a society whose members aspire to "white collar" jobs, and must "keep up with the Joneses" that these vices prevail. If you ask a man in India *what* he is, he will not say either that "I am a Brahman" or that "I am a Sudra" but that "I am a devotee of Krishna," or "I am a Saiva"; and that is not because he is either "proud" or "ashamed" of his caste, whatever it may be, but because he mentions first what seems to him more important than any social distinction.

For H. N. Brailsford (whose sincerity and courage I respect), author of *Subject India*, caste is indeed a "bugbear." It offends him that men's lives should be "hedged round from infancy by a network of prohibitions and commandments" and that "an Indian can become a Protestant or a rebel only by an effort of which none but the strongest natures are capable." He scarcely reflects that it may take a stronger nature to obey than to rebel; or that a strict pattern of "good form" is no more necessarily deplorable than is the fact that no one can compose a sonnet in free verse. Caste, he says, "makes of the individual a unit submissive in mind and body to a degree which startles and shocks the European observer," who is himself, of course, an "untouchable," and possibly a little "startled" by the implied disparagement. And yet, what admissions Mr. Brailsford makes when he comes to speak of caste in practice! One of the religious "prohibitions" or taboos ("save among the more degraded castes") is of drink. (The late Sister Nivedita once observed that Christianity "carries drunkenness in its wake"). But Mr. Brailsford tells us that "the Congress had Indian morality behind it when it organized a boycott of the government's toddy-shops . . . no Indian dare brave the condemnation of his fellows by entering them. In some places the all-powerful caste organization re-enforced the prohibition of Congress." You see that when it suits his argument, "prohibitions and commandments" become a "morality." There are other prohibitions and commandments that also pertain to *our* morality, and against which we do not feel called upon to "rebel or protest" against; and if there are some that he does not understand, has Mr. Brailsford ever thought of investigating their significance for us? Similarly in the case of the boycott of English manufactured goods he states, "its general success was an amazing proof of the solidarity of Indian society." How does he make that square with his statement that in India "by far the most serious obstacle to social unity comes from caste and its rule of endogamy?"[2]

Let us remember that in India men of different castes are divided neither by religion, culture, or language, but only by rules against intermarriage and interdining;[3] for example, no king could aspire to marry his own Brahman cook's daughter. That different castes have never found it difficult to work together for common ends is amply demonstrated by the almost universal institution of the *Pancayat*, or village council, a committee of men of different castes. Again, it may be observed that caste is not, in Hindu law, a legal disability; men of any caste may act as witnesses in suits, the only qualifications having to do with character and impartiality and being the same for all (*Manu* VIII, 61-63).

The Imperial Gazetteer remarks that the inhabitants of the typical Indian village "are welded together in a little community with its own organization and government . . . , its customary rules, and its little staff of functionaries, artisans and trades." Mr. Brailsford objects that "the only obstacles to the growth of internal trade on a gigantic scale is the poverty of the villages and the self-sufficiency that belongs to its oldest traditions . . . there is still many a village in which the hereditary craftsmen, who serve it for an allowance of grain, or some acres of free land, will weave all the cloth it needs, hammer its hoes for it and turn its pots." Unfortunately, "the growth of internal trade on a gigantic scale" is by no means one of our primary ambitions; we still hold (with Philo, *De Decalogo* 69) that it is an obvious truth that the craftsman is of higher value than the product of his craft, and perceive that it is chiefly in industrial societies that this truth is ignored; nor from what we know of factory conditions already existing in Bombay and elsewhere do we see the slightest prospect that the condition of even the lowest outcastes will ever be improved by a gigantic development of internal trade. Again, "we do not want the incredible American way of life."

---

[2] The cultural unity of India is emphasized even by Mr. Brailsford (p. 122). I should say that a much higher degree of "social unity" is realized in India than in the United States of America.

[3] It may be observed (1) that a Hindu does not "inter-dine" even with his own wife, or his own caste, and that this has nothing whatever to do with "social prejudice" of any kind, but reflects a functional differentiation; and (2) that the "prohibitions and commandments" of the caste system are not always so inconvenient as the superficial student supposes—for example, "From one's own ploughman, an old friend of the family, one's own cowherd, one's own servant, one's own barber, and from whomsoever else may come for refuge and offer service—from the hands of all such Sūdras food may be taken" (Manu VI. 253).

What we do see very clearly is that, in the words of A. M. Hocart, perhaps the only unprejudiced European sociologist who has written on caste, "hereditary service has been painted in such dark colours only because it is incompatible with the existing industrial system" (*Les castes*, p. 238).[4] Incompatible, because caste involves human relationships and mutual responsibilities for which there is no room in a world of capital and labour and manufacture for profit on the one hand or in the Soviet types of collective organization on the other. No type of civilization can be accepted that does not provide for the worker's happiness: and no man can be happy who is forced to earn a living otherwise than by the labours for which he is naturally fitted and to which therefore he can literally devote himself with enthusiasm. I say that no man *can* be happy but in "that station of life to which it has pleased God to call him"; that man is literally *unfortunate* (deprived of his due inheritance) if either the state or his own ambition bring it about that his fortune and his nature are incongruous—"*d'un vrai travail on ne peut pas se débarrasser, c'est la vie même.*"

What we said above on village organization ought to have made it clear that the traditional government of India is far less centralized and far less bureaucratic than any form of government known to the modern democracies. One might, indeed, say that the castes are the stronghold of a self-government far more real than could be achieved by any counting of the noses of all the millions of a proletariat. To a very large extent the caste group coincides with the trade guild; and before the impact of industrialism and *laissez faire*, and especially in the great cities, these trade guilds exercised very many of the functions that the bureaucracies now undertake with far less efficiency, and some that the bureaucracies scarcely attempt to fulfill. Thus, apart from their function of maintaining standards of quality both as to materials and workmanship, and providing for education through apprenticeship (or, rather, the master-and-disciple relationship), they covered the whole field of

---

[4] Similarly Mr. Brailsford (p. 160): "The caste line will have to be broken, *if* industrial work is to be provided for the superfluous cultivators" (italics mine).

On the other hand, in his excellent book *Dharma and Society* (London, 1935), G. H. Mees remarks that "no serious student of caste will propagate the abolishment of the caste system" (p. 192). It will not be overlooked that Mahatma Gandhi himself, so well known as a champion of the "untouchables," does not wish to do away with caste.

See also Bhavān Dās, *The Science of Social Organization* (Madras, 1910), pp. 226 and 335). "Manu's scheme is the nearest and only approach to a workable socialism that has been tried in our race, and that succeeded for thousands of years."

charity and what is now known as that of "social security." One might say that if India was not in the Chinese or Islamic sense a democratic country, it was nevertheless a land of many democracies, i.e. self-governing groups in full control of all matters really falling within their competence; and that perhaps no other country in the world has been better trained in self-government. But, as Sir George Birdwood said, "under British rule in India, the authority of the trade guilds has necessarily been relaxed"; the nature of such a "necessity" will hardly bear analysis.

There are types of society that are by no means "above," but on the contrary "below" caste; societies in which there prevails what the traditional sociologies term a "confusion of castes"; societies in which men are regarded primarily if not, indeed, exclusively as economic animals, and the expression "standard of living," dear to the advertising manufacturer, has only quantitative connotations. Such societies as these have, indeed, "progressed" toward, and perhaps attained to "the pure and 'inorganic' multiplicity of a kind of social atomism, and to the exercise of a purely mechanical activity in which nothing properly human subsists so that a man can adopt any profession or even change it at will as if this profession were something purely exterior to himself" (René Guénon).[5] The mere existence of these great proletarian aggregates, whose members, exploited by one another, pullulate in "capitals" that have no longer any organic connection with the bodies on which they grew, but depend on world markets that must be opened by "wars of pacification" and continually stimulated by the "creation of new wants" by suggestive advertisement, is destructive of the more highly differentiated traditional societies in which the individual has a status determined by his function and in no sense merely by wealth or poverty; their existence is automatically destructive of the individual whom its "efficiency" reduces to the level of a producer of raw materials, destined to be worked up in the victor's factories, and again unloaded upon the "backward" peoples who must accept their annual quota of gadgets, if business is to prosper.[6] Even such a good "progressive" as Mr. Brailsford is forced to ask whether man "is not too wicked to be trusted with powerful machines!"

The economic results of commercial exploitation ("world trade")

---

[5] For René Guénon and his work, which is of so much significance from the standpoint of "Synthesis," see my "Eastern Wisdom and Western Knowledge" in *Isis*, Vol. XXXIV, (1943), pp. 359-363. (Also published in *Am I My Brother's Keeper*, John Day: New York, 1947).

[6] "After this war, England must increase her exports 50 per cent over 1938" (from a speech by Lord Keynes, 1942). Commentary: "The American Revolution was in main a revolt against mercantilism" (R. L. Buell, editor of *Fortune*).

are typically summarized in Albert Schweitzer's words, "whenever the timber trade is good, permanent famine reigns in the Ogowe region." When thus "commerce settles on every tree," the spiritual consequences are even more devastating; "civilization" can destroy the souls as well as the bodies of those whom it infects. Of course, I am aware that there are plenty of Westernized Orientals who are perfectly willing and even anxious to welcome the *dona ferentes* of industry without for a moment hesitating to examine these gift horses; but strange as it may appear to the Wallaces who would like to "get (us) started on the path of industrialism," it is precisely from the standpoint of the caste system that an Indian can most confidently and effectively criticize modern Western civilization.

Among the most severe of these critics are to be found some of those deceptively Westernized Orientals who have themselves lived and studied longest in Europe and America. To such people it is clear that, in the undifferentiated social antheaps of the Western world, the "common man" finds his labours so detestable that he is always hankering after a "leisure state"; that this "common man" is in fact a mass product in a world of uniform mass productions and universal compulsory "education"; that the "collective wisdom of a literate (western) people" is little better than a collective ignorance; and that there can be no comparison between the proletarian "common man" of the West with the cultured but illiterate peasant of the traditional "community whose intellectual interests are the same from the top of the social structure to the bottom" (G. L. Kittredge). He sees that it is precisely in the most "individualistic" societies that the fewest individuals are to be found.[7] It certainly does not surprise him to find native observers saying that in the West "there remains the show of civilization, without any of its realities" (A. N. Whitehead), or admitting that "while inventions and mechanical devices have been developed to a tremendous extent, there has been no moral or spiritual development among men to equal that process" (J. C. Hambro); describing modern society as a "murderous machine, with no conscience, and no ideals" (G. La Piana), or recognizing that "civilization, as we now have it, can only end in disaster" (G. H. Estabrooks). Just *what* is it that you, who are so conscious of your "civilizing mission," have to offer us? Can you wonder that, as Rabindranath Tagore said, "there is no people in the whole of Asia which does not look upon Europe with fear and suspicion" or that we dread the prospect of an alliance of the imperialistic powers whose "Atlantic Charter" was not meant to

---

[7] *"Ce que l'Etat moderne craint le plus, c'est l'individu"* (Jean Giono, *Lettre aux Paysans*, (1938), p. 64).

132 THE BUGBEAR OF LITERACY

apply to India, and will not be applied to China if it can be avoided? An aphorism several times repeated in Buddhist scripture runs, "war breeds hatred, because the conquered are unhappy"; and that is even more true of economic than of military wars, for in the former no holds whatever are barred, and there are no truces of any intention to make peace.

In any discussion of the caste system, just as would be the case if it were a matter of kingship,* we have always to deal with a host of errors that are constantly repeated even by otherwise well-informed Western writers. One of the chief of these is a view that is stated as a fact by the authors of *Twentieth Century India* (Institute of Pacific Relations, 1944, p. 17), viz., that: "The caste system is peculiar to Hinduism." On this subject let me quote Hocart again: He says in his Preface that something at least will have been accomplished "if the reader can be persuaded that the Indian caste system is not, as is generally believed, an isolated phenomenon, but belongs to a widely diffused social-category (*genre*). And since it is not an isolated phenomenon, it cannot be understood if we isolate it," Rather less than half of his book has to do with India; the remainder deals with Persia, the Hebrews, South Sea Islands, Greece, and Egypt, and one may add that considerable space might have been given to Japan and to the feudal system in Europe.[9] All we can say

---

* References to the "absolute monarchies" of the Orient are continually repeated, as if these monarchies could be compared to that of France immediately before the revolution. There have been, of course, good and bad kings there, as everywhere else. The normal Oriental monarchy is really a theocracy. in which the king's position is that of an executive who may do only what ought to be done and is a servant of justice (*dharma*) of which he is not himself the author. The whole prosperity of the state depends upon the king's virtue; and just as for Aristotle, the monarch who rules in his own interests is not a king but a tyrant, and may be removed "like a mad dog," According to the old Hindu law, a king is to be fined a thousand times as much as a Sūdra for the same offense. It is in a very different way that one observes in the democracies "one law for the rich and another for the poor." What we see in a democracy governed by "representatives" is not a government "for the people" but an organized conflict of *interests* that only results in the setting up of unstable balances of power; and that "while the tyranny of one is cruel, that of many cannot but be most harsh and intolerable" (Philo, *Spec.* IV. 113). So just as an Oriental criticizes the industrial system by his own vocational standards, so he criticizes democracy by his ideal of kingship. See further my *Spiritual Authority and Temporal Power in the Indian Theory of Government* (1942), for India especially, p. 86; for Persia, note 60.

Similarly T. W. Rhys Davids in *Sacred Books of the Buddhists*, II. 96 f: "Evidence has been yearly accumulating on the existence of restrictions as to intermarriage, and as to the right of eating together, among other Aryan tribes—Greeks, Germans, Russians and so on. Both the spirit, and to a is that in India the vocational structure of society has been more strongly emphasized, and has longer survived intact than elsewhere. Another error is that of the scholars who attribute the caste system in India to the enslavement of the darker indigenous races by blonde conquerors. It suffices to point out, as Hocart has, that the four castes are connected with the four quarters and are of four "colours" —white, red, yellow, and black—and that to be consistent, the ethnic theory ought to have presupposed invaders of three separate colours, a white race becoming the priests, a red race the rulers, and a yellow race the merchants of the invaded territory! The only real colour distinction is between the three and the one, the colours in question being respectively those of day and night, or "gold" and "iron"; in the divine operation the Supreme Identity assumes now the one, now the other, at will. The distinction is only partially reflected in the sensible world; the actual colour of Indian peoples varies from blonde to black, and it is by no means the case that all Brahmins are blonde or that all Sūdras are black.

The word Brahmana is a patronymic from Brahma (God); the "true" Brahman, as distinguished from the "Brahman-by-birth" is the "knower of Brahma." In the sacrificial myth we are told that the Brahman is "born from the mouth" of the Divine Person; and that this implies a second birth (members of the three upper castes are all *dvija*, "twice-born") is clear from the fact that even the child of a Brahman family receives only an existence from his parents, and is no better than a Sudra before his birth of the Veda (*Manu* II, 147, 172); he only becomes a Brahman properly to be so called when he has been initiated by Brahman teacher, who represents the Progenitor *in divinis*, and of whom he is reborn "from his mouth" (*Satapatha Brahmana* XI. 5.4.1).[10] So we find a man who has studied the scriptures at the feet of a competent teacher described in the *Chandogya Upanisad* as "shining like a Brahma-knower," and that is what it really means to be of the "Brahmana complexion" (*Varna*). The two Indian words for "caste" are *varna* (colour) and *jati* (birth).[11]

---

large degree, the actual details of modern Indian caste usages, are identical with these ancient, and no doubt universal customs."

[10] The distinctions cited above make the Buddhist polemic of *Mujjhima* Nikāya II, 148 ridiculous.

The modern Western reader to whom the notion of a ritual second birth may be strange should study the second chapter of Dionysius' *Ecclesiastical Hierarchy*, e.g., in Darboy's version. *Saint Denys l'Areopagite* (Paris, 1932), pp. 83-91).

[11] "*Ce mot jāti signifie literalement 'naissance,' mais il ne faudrait l'entendre, ou du moins pas exclusivement ni en principe, au sens d'hérédité; il designe la nature individuelle de l'etre, en tant qu'elle est necessairement determinee*

Of these two, *varna*, from a root meaning to "cover" or "conceal" means a good deal more than just "colour" or "complexion"; it means an appearance, individuality or character that a given essence may assume; *varna* and *jati* are not synonymous but normally concomitant. In a Buddhist context we find a Brahmana explaining that a Brahman is such who is of pure descent (*jati*), knowledge of scripture, flowerlike complexion (*varna-pushkaratā*), virtuous (*sīlavat*) and cultured (*pandita*); but of these five qualifications, only the two last are indispensable.

It will be necessary now to consider the origin, nature, and implications of the caste system, mainly in India. This we shall attempt entirely from an Indian point of view, and quite independently of the conflicting, changeable, and often prejudiced theories of the Western sociologists. In the first place, it must be understood that the terms of the hierarchical classifications are applicable not merely to human beings but *in divinis* and throughout the universe.[12] We must begin with the great distinction of the gods (*Devas, Aryas*) and Titans (*Asuras, Anaryas*) who are nevertheless brothers, and children of a common father. The distinction is as of day from night, or light from darkness, and in this sense, one of colour (*varna*); the opposition is due to the fact that the Titans are the original possessors of the Source of Life and of the Light and of the world itself, all of which must be wrested from them if there is to be a world in which gods and men shall be enabled to fulfill their destiny.

The power of exercising all function whatever inheres in the unity of the primordial World-Man or Divine Person, the *Purusha*, who is so called because in every political body, whether collective or individual, he is the essential *citizen*,[13] just as for Philo the deity is μόνος πολιτικός [*monos politicos*]. From the sacrificial division of his functions, at the same time that having been one he becomes a plurality of citizens, arise the two groups of the four castes, Brahmana, Kshatriya, Vaishya and Sūdra, by a distribution of

---

des sa naissance meme, comme l'ensemble des possibilités qu'il développera au cours de son existence." (René Guénon, "Varna," in *Le Voile d'Isis*, Vol. 40 (1935), p. 447). Heredity, that is to say, is normally the largest factor in determining an individual's possibilities; but even where a character arises as it were spontaneously, it is still, in the sense that we speak of, "a born poet," a "birth" that defines the individual's possibilities.

12   See especially *Taittirīya Samhitā*, VII.1.1-3 and *Aitareya Brāhmana*, VIII. 4 where the four castes originating from the mouth, arms, thighs and feet of the Sacrifice correspond to the four lauds of the Agnistoma and the qualities of brilliance, strength, fertility, and support.

13   *Pur* = πολις *polis*, the root appearing also in *plures, plebs*, people, fill, etc; *sha* = κείμαι [*Keimai*], *cubare*.

qualities and functions (*Rgveda* X. 90, *Bhagavad Gita* IV. 13, etc). The classes of the gods are those of the Sacerdotium, (Regnum and Commons corresponding to the three first of the castes just mentioned), while the Asuras are the Sudras.[14]

Humanly speaking, the hierarchy of the castes is the same. It is not a hierarchy of races, but of functions and of standards and ways of living. Very many things are allowed a Sudra which a Brahman may not do. In law, for the same offense, a Brahman's punishment is to be sixty-four times that of a Sudra. We are not for a moment pretending that the untouchability of the lower and (out-)castes, which is so offensive to modern minds, is in any sense an excrescence upon the caste system; neither shall we defend it by a citation of English or American parallels, since two wrongs would not make a right, and in any case we are not apologizing for, but rather explaining the caste system. Nor, indeed, would such a comparison be really valid; for the caste taboos are not based upon racial or colour prejudice as such (a fallen Brahman, however well-born or fair, is under the same disabilities as an outcaste by birth, *Manu* XI, 245, 98, etc), but are for the sake of the preservation of a ritual purity at once physical and psychic. I wonder, sometimes, if foreign reformers ever realize that if we should admit the Indian outcastes to our temple sanctuaries, we might as well admit Europeans? Actually, just as the Titans are by all means excluded from the sacrifices offered by the Gods, so are Sūdras from participation in the cults of the higher castes (*Taittirīya Samhitā* VII, 1.1.6). At least as early as the eighth century B.C. (*Śatapatha Brāhmana* XI, 1.1.31), we find that the teacher of an esoteric doctrine, which may not be taught to anyone and everyone, but only to the qualified,[15] may neither touch nor even look at a Sūdra. But this does not mean that the lower castes, or even the outcaste, is in any way deprived of a religion. In the first place, he has cults of his own, intimately connected with his own *metier*, and these are by no means extraneous to, but only a phase of, Hinduism as a whole; distinctions of cult in India are not a matter of "other gods," but of convenience; the way of works and of devotion is open to all, and actually not a few of India's greatest saints have been of Sūdra or even Chandāla

---

[14] It has been maintained by many Western scholars that apart from the "late" hymn (*Rgveda* X. 90) the *Rgveda* knows only of three castes. But the equation Sūdra = Asura (explicit in *Taittirīya Brāhmana* 1.2.6.7) would need no demonstration to an Indian. It is, indeed, precisely because Asura = Sūdra that the Soma from which the ritual "ambrosia" is prepared must be "purchased" from a Sūdra.

[15] Cf. *Matthew* 7 : 6, *Luke* 8 : 10; Dionysius, *Ecclesiastical Hierarchy* VI, 2; St. Thomas Aquinas, *Exp. s. Boetium De Trinitate* II.4.

136THE BUGBEAR OF LITERACY

birth. Nor can we ignore the case of the "mother-son" who comes, as is told in the *Chandogya Upanisad*, to a Brahmana teacher, to be his disciple. He is asked of what family he is, and can only answer that he is the son of his mother, and cannot possibly say who his father may have been: the Brahmana accepts him, on the ground that such candor is tantamount to Brahman lineage, and withholds nothing of his doctrine, so that he in turn becomes a "knower of God" and a teacher of disciples of his own.

However, we are not so much concerned here with the secular history of caste as a social institution as with its spiritual significance. At the back of all Indian metaphysics lies the conception that the existent world in all its variety originates in a primordial differentiation of one into many;[16] and that it can only be preserved in a state of well-being by an "extension of the thread of the sacrifice," i.e., by its ritual perpetuation, whereby the process of creation is continued;[17] just as a human "line" can only be extended by a perpetuation of father-mother relationships which are also to be regarded as ritual acts. Now the archetypal sacrificer is often called the "All-worker" (*visva-karman*), and its human mimesis in fact demands a cooperation of all the skills that men possess, or in other words that of all kinds of men (since, in vocational societies, the artist is not a special kind of man, but every man a special kind of artist).

Hence, if the sacrifice (i.e. in Christian terms, the Mass) is to be correctly, that is, perfectly performed—which is essential to the success of its purpose, which are those of present well-being and future beatitude—the sacrificial society must include all kinds of artists.[18] In this sense it is literally true that, as the Indian phrase would run, the vocations are "born of the sacrifice." Conversely, the vocations themselves are "sanctified"; and even when the craftsman is working for the benefit of other men and not obviously to provide the essentials of a divine service, his operation (*karman*) is a rite, as in *Rgveda* IX. 11d, 1 where the works of priests, physicians, and carpenters are all alike *vratani*. One might add with reference to the "free" *actus primus* in which the idea of the thing to be made

---

[16] The diety is *one* transcendentally "there," but *many* as he is immanent in his children "here" *Satapatha Brāhmana* X.5.2.16).

[17] On the "circulation of the shower of wealth" for which the sacrificial order provides, see *Satapatha Brāhmana* IX.3.3.15-19 and my *Spiritual Authority and Temporal Power*, p. 68 and note 50.

[18] In the traditional and legitimate, rather than the current sense of the word, "the concept of the artist, and the related concept of the fine arts are both special bad accidents of our own local European tradition." (Margaret Mead).

is conceived in an imitable form, before the "servile" *actus secundus* of manual operation is undertaken, that the artist may be called, like any other contemplative *dhira, yogi,* or *sadhaka,* and that the inconographic prescriptions of the technical books are referred to as *dhyana mantrams,* i.e., contemplative formulas.

Illustrations of the sacred quality of the traditional arts could be cited from India and many other cultures; for example, Japan, where a "carpenter still builds according to Shinto tradition: he dons a priestly costume at a certain stage of his work, performs rites, and chants invocations, and places the new house under the protection of the gods. But the occupation of the swordsmith was in old days the most sacred of the crafts: he worked in priestly garb, and practised Shinto rites of purification while engaged in the making of a good blade. Before his smithy was then suspended the rope of rice straw, which is the oldest symbol of Shinto; none even of his family might enter there, or speak to him; and he ate only of food cooked with holy fire" (Lafcadio Hearn, *Japan,* 1905, p. 169). Similarly, in the Marquesas Islands, when a new canoe was to be built, liturgical service is first performed in which the whole of the work is referred to the archetypal process of creation; and while the work itself is being carried on, the craftsmen and their assistants live and work together in a sacred precinct protected by *tabus,* observing a strict continence and cooking their own food (W. C. Handy, *L'Art des Iles Marquises,* 1938). It will be self-evident that while, from the missionary point of view, all such "superstitious practices" must be suppressed in the interests of their own "true religion" (and, in fact, the French, in the course of their *oeuvre civilisatrice,* have forbidden them), they are quite "incompatible with the existing industrial system, and must be abandoned if the Marquesas Islanders are to "progress." It might be no exaggeration to say that modern civilization is fundamentally a "racket"; needless to name the gangsters.

The traditional arts and crafts are, in fact, "mysteries," with "secrets" that are not merely "tricks of the trade" of economic value (like the so-much-abused European "patents"), but pertain to the worldwide and immemorial symbolism of the techniques, all of which are analogies or imitations of the creative nature in operaion:[19] the universe itself, for example, being a "tissue" of which the

---

[19] With this scholastic formula, cf. *Aitareya Brāhmaṇa* V. 27, where we are told that human works of art are made in imitation of celestial paradigms and the artist is described as "visiting heaven" (a reference to the primary act of contemplation) in order to observe the forms that he will, upon his return, embody in the material. "Wisdom" αοφίο *sophia,* cf. the Sanskrit *kauśalyam*) was originally the maker's "skill." Analogies from the con-

warp threads are formal rays of the uncreated image-bearing light, the woof the primary matter in contact with which the aforesaid illumination becomes a colour, and the pattern their progeny. The knowledge of these analogies is that of the "lesser mysteries," and these are a property of the *metier* into which an apprentice is not simply admitted, but "initiated."[20]

Let us now turn for a moment to the word *karman* which has been cited above. The meanings of the verbal root *kar*, present also in the Latin *creare* and the Greek κραίνω [*kraino*], are to make, do, and effect. And significantly, just as the Latin *facere* is originally *sacra facere*, literally "make sacred," and as the Greek ποιέω -- ἱεροποιέω [*poieo hieropoieo*], so *karman* is originally and very often not merely "work" or "making," but synonymous with *vajña*, "sacrifice" and also with *vrata*, "sacred operation," "obedience," "sphere of activity," "function," and especially as in the *Bhagavad Gita*, with *dharma*, "justice" or "natural law." In other words, the idea is deeply rooted in our humanity that there is no real distinction of work from holy works, and no necessary opposition of profane to sacred activities. And it is precisely this idea that finds such vivid expression in the well-known Indian philosophy of action, the "Way of Works" (*karma-mārga*) of the *Bhagavad Gita*.

In the following citations from the *Bhagavad Gita*, it must be understood that while we render *karma* by "action," it is actually impossible to make any essential distinction of the meaning "sacrificial operation" for that of "operation" or "duty." This is, indeed, in full agreement with several texts of the Upanisads in which all the activities of life are sacrificially interpreted. It is precisely such an "interpretation," by which activities are referred to their paradigms *in divinis*, that marks the difference between the Comprehensor (*evamvit*) and the mere behaviorist. *Siddhi*, rendered by "perfection," is a hard word to translate; the root implies the achievement of whatever ends one has in view, also to be set right,

---

structive arts are notably absent from the writings of modern philosophers, but abound in those of ancient, mediaeval and oriental philosophers, who are still masters of *"le symbolisme qui sait."* It is of these analogies that St. Bonaventura remarks, "Behold, how the light of a mechanical art is the path to the illumination of Holy Scripture! There is nothing therein that does not bespeak a true wisdom (*sapientia = scientia cum amore"*), and it is for this reason that Holy Scripture very properly makes frequent use of such similes" (*De reductione artium ad theologiam*, 14). It is just that sort of "wisdom" that cannot be found where manufacture is only for profit, and not primarily for use.

[20] Cf. René Guénon, "Initiation and the Crafts," *Journal of the Indian Society of Oriental Art*, Vol. VI (1938).

to be healed or matured; the sense in our contexts is as nearly as possible that of the Greek τελείωσις [*teleiosis*]. With these premises, we cite from this Indian sermon as follows:[21]

> The 'four colours' arise from Me, who am the distributor of qualities and actions. The activities proper to each have been distributed according to the qualities that predominate in the nature (*sva-bhāva*) of each. There is nothing whatever in this whole universe that I needs must do, naught that I lack or might obtain that is not already mine; and yet I participate in action. Else would these worlds upset, and I should be the author of "confusion of colours" and a destroyer of my children. So even as the ignorant act, because of their attachment to activity, so should the Comprehensor act, but without attachment for the holding-together of the world.[22] "Skill" in actions is what is meant by "yoking" (yoga).[23] Better is one's own-duty (*sva-dharma*), however mean, than that of others, however highly praised. Better to die in the doing of one's own duty (than to desert); another's duty is a fearsome thing! He who is a doer of actions determined by his own-nature (*sva-bhāva*) incurs no sin. One should never abandon the work to which one is born (*sahajam karma*). For man reaches perfection when each is in love with (*abhi-ratah*) his own work. It finds perfection in that in his own work he is praising Him from whom is the sending forth of all beings and by whom all this universe has been extended *Laborare est orare.*

In other words, everyman's Way to become what he is—what he has it in him to become—is one of perfectionism in that station of life to which his own nature (i.e. nativity) imperiously summons him. The pursuit of perfection is everyman's "equality of opportunity"; and the goal is the same for all, for the miner and the professor alike, because there are no degrees of perfection. This

---

[21] The verses cited are II. 50; III. 22, 24, 25, 35; IV. 12; XVIII. 41, 45-48, but in a different order.

[22] Just as in the *Republic*, 519G ff., where those who have seen the light, and would not willingly partake in the activities of the "cave," are nevertheless expected to "go down again" καταβαίνειν [*katabainein   avatartum*] and to participate in them, for the sake of the other cave-dwellers, but unlike them in having no ends of their own to be attained, no personal motives. "Holding together" (*samgrahana*) corresponds exactly to Plato's (519E).

[23] "Yoga" here in its primary sense, with reference to the control of the sense powers by the governing mind (in the Indian and Platonic-Philonic symbolism of the chariot, i.e., bodily vehicle of the spirit, the sense-powers being the team of horses). If we are also told in the *Bhagavad Gita* that "the renunciation of actions is what is meant by "yoking," there is no contradiction, because this is explicitly *not* a repudiation of activity but implies the reference of all activities not to oneself but to the veritable Agent whose *instruments* we only are. The work will be done the more easily and the more "skillfully" the less it is referred to our self, and the more we let Him act through us. It is not an idleness, but a facility that the "action without activity" of the *Bhagavad Gita*, and the corresponding Taoist *wu wei* intend.

whole point of view is already implicit in the old equation *karma* =
yajña, i.e., *facere* = *sacra facere*. For it is again and again insisted
upon in the ritual texts that the Sacrifice must be *perfectly* performed
—nothing too little or too much— if the sacrificer's purpose is to be
attained; and this of course implies that whatever is done in or made
for the Sacrifice must be perfectly done or made. It is a striking
illustration of this perfectionism (and one that vividly reminds us
of the Shaker philosophy of work) that in a Buddhist context
(*Anguttara Nikāya*, 111, 363) in which the entelechies of the monk,
ruler,   and   householder,   etc.,   are   defined,   the   "fulfillment"
(*pariyosāna*) of the householder, whose means of livelihood is the
practice of an art, is "perfected workmanship." In the words of
St. Thomas Aquinas, "the craftsman is *naturally* inclined by *justice*
to do his work faithfully" (*Summa Theologica* I-II, 57, 3 *ad* 2).

The modern mind, it may be observed, is not opposed to the
concept of vocation *per se*; in the absence of an established heredity
of functions, it sets up, on the contrary, "vocational tests" and seeks
to provide for a guidance in the "choice of a vocation." What it
most of all resents is the hereditary principle, which seems to set an
arbitrary limit to the individual's equality of opportunity. This
resentment is natural enough in the case of a proletarian society in
which a confusion of castes has already taken place, and where the
constitution of traditional civilization based on first principles and
"in which all is ordered and in a hierarchy consistent with these
principles" (Réne Guénon) can hardly be imagined.

As to this, let us say in the first place that while such principles
are immutable in themselves, their application to circumstances of
time and place is contingent, or, rather, a matter of convenience
(using this excellent term in its strict sense). Accordingly, if one
were to imagine a caste system imposed upon the existing American
scene, it would not necessarily have to be a hereditary system, if it
were really provided for that even a majority of men could earn
their living by doing what they would rather be doing than anything
else in the world;[24] if the workman's unions were at once ready and
able to insist upon the workman's human responsibility both for the
production of the necessaries of life, and for their quality. Even
supposing that the traditional caste systems in practice fall short, or
for the sake of argument very far short of their theory, would it not
be better if the social reformer, instead of attacking a theory (of
which he very rarely has any real understanding) were to ask himself whether the traditional systems were not in fact designed to
realize a kind of social justice that *cannot* be realized in any com-

[24] In even more popular terms, if men could live by what are now only
their hobbies.

petative industrial system where all production is primarily for profit, where the consumer is a "guinea pig," and where for all but a fortunate few, occupation is *not* a matter of free choice, but economically, and in that sense arbitrarily, determined?[25] It is not, then, to apologize for the caste system, but to explain it, that we write, in the hope that the reader will put such questions as these to himself.

Let us, then, explain the significance of the hereditary principle in a society in which the castes are not yet confused. The inheritance of functions is a matter of re-birth—*not* in the current misinterpretation of the word, but as rebirth is defined in Indian scriptures and in accordance with the traditional assumption that *the father himself is reborn in his son.* We have seen that the function is "born of the sacrifice," and this means that if the needs of the theocentric society are to be met, the ministerial functions by which the dual purposes of the sacrifice (well-being here and beatitude hereafter) are to be secured must be perpetuated from generation to generation; the function is at once an estate and an incumbency and, as such, entailed. Just as for Plato and in Scholastic philosophy, so for the Vedânta, *duo sunt in homine,* and of these two, one is the mortal personality or character of this man, so-and-so, the other, the immortal part and very person of the man himself.[26] It is only to the former, individual nature that the category of "colour" can be applied; the word *varna* itself could, indeed, be rendered not inaccurately by "individuality," inasmuch as colour arisen from the contact of light with a material, which then exhibits a colour that is determined not by the light, but by its own nature.

"My" individuality or psychophysical constitution is not, from this point of view, an end in itself either for me or for others, but always a means, garment, vehicle or tool to be made good use of for as and for so long as it is "mine"; it is not an absolute, but only a relative value, personal insofar as it can be utilized as means to the attainment of man's last end of liberation (*Bhagavad Gita,* V. 11), and social in its adaptation to the fulfilment of this, that, or the other specialized function. It is the individuality, and not the person, that is bequeathed by the father to his son, in part by heredity, in part

---

[25] "We live as if economic forces determined the growth and decay of institutions and settled the fate of individuals. Liberty becomes a well-nigh obsolete term; we start, go, and stop at the signal of a vast industrial machine" (J. Dewey, *The Individualism Old and New* (1931), p. 12.

[26] This is a discrimination that may be more familiar to the reader in the Christian terms of the distinction of our outer from our inner man, or "sundering of soul from spirit." For a further analysis see my "*Akimcanna, self-naughting,*" in New Indian Antiquary, Vol. III (1940). (Also in "*Selected Writings of Ananda Coomaraswamy*" Princeton Univ. Press, 1977).

THE BUGBEAR OF LITERACY

by example, and in part by formal rites of transmission: when the father becomes *emeritus*, or at his death, the son inherits his position, and, in the widest sense of the word, his debts, i.e., social responsibilities. This acceptance of the paternal inheritance sets the father free from the burden of social responsibility that attached to him as an individual; "having done what there was for him to do," the very man departs in peace. It is not, then, for our mere pleasure or pride that children are to be begotten; indeed, they will be "no children of ours" if they do not in their turn assume our burden of responsibilities—"Children are begotten in order that there may be a succession of sacrificial-functionaries"—"for the perpetuation of these worlds" (*Satapatha Brāhmana* I, 8 1.31; *Aitareya Upanisad* IV. 4), and just as in India, so for Plato, "Concerning marriage, it is decreed that we should adhere to the ever-productive nature by providing servants of God in our own stead; and this we do by always leaving behind us children's children" (*Laws*, 774 A).

It is only in the light of the doctrine of the two selves and the no less universal imperative to "Know thyself" (to know, that is, which of these two selves is our very Self), that we can really understand the resentment of "prohibitions and commandments" and of "inequality" and the corresponding advocacy of "protest and rebellion" that we spoke of above. That resentment has far deeper roots than are to be found in the mere fact of an existing confusion of castes, which should be regarded much rather as a symptom than as a primary cause of disorder.

An impatience of restraints is not in itself reprehensible, but natural to every prisoner. The traditional concept of liberty goes far beyond, in fact, the demand of any anarchist; it is the concept of an absolute, unfettered freedom to be as, when, and where we will. All other and contingent liberties, however desirable and right, are derivative and to be valued only in relation to this last end. But this conception of an absolute liberty is coupled with the assured conviction that of all possible restraints upon it by far the strictest is that of a subjection to whatever-is-not-ourself, and most notably within this category, that of a subjection to the desires and passions of our outer man, the "individual." When, now, like Boethius, we have "forgotten who we are" and, identifying ourselves with our outer man, have become "lovers of our own selves," then we transfer to him all our longing to be free, and imagine that our whole happiness will be contained in *his* freedom to go his own way and find pasture where he will. There, in ignorance and in desire, lie the roots of "individualism" and of what we call in India "the law of the sharks," and in America "free enterprise." Whoever proposes to discontent the members of a traditional society (whose present "submissiveness" annoys him) with what is rightly called their "lot" must realize that he will only be able to do so to the extent that he is able to impose on them his own conviction of the identity of his ego with himself.

In the same way, when it is asserted that "all men are born equal," of what "men" are we speaking? The statement is evidently untrue of all "outer men," for we see that they are both physically and mentally differently endowed and that natural aptitudes have to be considered even in nominally egalitarian societies. A predication of equality is only absolutely true of *all inner men*; true of the men themselves, but not of their personalities. Accordingly, in the *Bhagavad Gita* itself (V. 18) where, as we have already seen, the validity of caste distinction is strongly emphasized, and a confusion of castes is tantamount to the death of a society, it is also taught that "the true philosopher (*pandit*) is *same-sighted* towards a Brahman perfected in wisdom and conduct, towards a cow, or an elephant, or even a dog or an eater of dogs," i.e., a *Chandāla*, or "outcaste." *Same-sighted*, untouched by likes or dislikes: this does not mean that he is unaware of inequalities among the "outer men" to whom the categories of the social system really apply, and who are still burdened with rights and duties; it means that as a perfected seer, one who has himself risen above all distinctions established by natural qualities (as all men may), and is no longer of the world, he is colour-blind, and sees nothing but the ultimate and colourless essence, immortal and divine, and "equal" because unmodified and undivided, not only in every man, but in every living creature "down to the ants."

Our object in bringing forward these considerations (which it would hardly occur to a modern sociologist to deal with in any social analysis) is to make it perfectly clear that, just as in criticizing a work of art we cannot isolate the object of our study from its total environment without "killing" it, so in the case of any given custom, we cannot expect to understand its significance for those whose custom it is, if we vivisect the society in which it flourishes, and so extract a "formula" which we then proceed to criticize *as if* it were to be forthwith imposed upon ourselves by *force majeure*. The parts of a traditional society are not merely aggregated in it, but co-ordinated; its elements are fitted together like the parts of a jigsaw puzzle; and it is only when and where the whole picture can be seen that we can know what we are talking about. Wholes are immanent in *all* their parts; and the parts are intelligible only in the context of the whole.

The reader may have noticed above that the *Bhagavad Gita* in commending the caste system also speaks of the worker's "delight" in his work; the word employed, *abhi-rata* (*ram* with an intensifying prefix), might as well have been rendered by "being in love with,"

as if with a bride; a fundamental sense of the root is to "come to
rest in," as desire comes to rest in its object, when this has been
attained. The craftsman, under normal conditions, likes nothing
better than to talk about his work. We cannot but regard as
abnormal the condition of the chain-belt worker who would rather
talk about anything but his work; his deep interest is not in the
work, in the doing of which he is little more than an irresponsible
instrument of the "manufacturer" for profit, but in racing, baseball,
films, or other means of entertainment or diversion.[27] It could not
be said of such as these that their work is their "rest," or that an
Eros or Muse inspires them. In a vocational society, on the other
hand, it is taken for granted that "everyone is very proud of his
hereditary science" (kula-vidyā, Kālidāsa, Mālavikāgnim mitra 1.4).
So, Philo, pointing out that when the king asks,"What is your work?"
he receives the answer, "We are shepherds, as were our fathers"
(Genesis 47: 3), comments: "Aye, indeed! Does it not seem that
they were more proud of being shepherds than is the king, who is
talking to them, of his sovereign power?" (Agr. 59, 60). In one of
Dekker's plays, he makes his grocer express the fervent wish, May
no son of mine ever be anything but a grocer![28] As Jean Giono says,
apropos of overtime, that as things are "les ouvriers font quarante
heures de travail par semain. Je voudrais bien qu'ils ne fassent point
d'heure du tout, quitte à leur gré a faire cent heures d'un travail qui
leur passionerait" (Lettre aux Paysans, p. 37). Moi, je le veux aussi!
Passionerait: I have known hereditary craftsmen in Ceylon,

---

[27] "These workers look on labour as a necessary evil, as an opportunity to
earn money which wilyl enable them not only to supply their essential needs
but also to treat themselves to luxuries and give free rein to their passions"
A. J. Krzesinski, Is Modern Culture Doomed? (1942), p. 54. "It matters
not whether the present-day factory-worker is, as regards the duration and
intensity of his exertion, in a better or worse condition than the savage
hunter or the artisan of the Middle Ages. The point that does matter is
that his mind has no share in determining the aims of his work and that
his body, as an instrument of independent creative power, has lost most
of its significance . . . and now (work) interests him almost exclusively
as a source of pleasure and discomfort" (ibid., p. 54, note 8). Pleasure and
discomfort—the very "pairs" from the domination of which the Indian and
Platonic philosophers would liberate us! It would be absurd, indeed, to
pretend that modern society is not based upon and supported by slave labour;
it is only the name of slavery and not its reality that is repudiated.
[28] Synonymous with the sahajam karma of Bhagavad Gita, cited above, and
with the householder's sippa in Anguttara Nikāya, III. 363, where we are
told that this man's concern is for wealth, his domain an art (sippādhitthāna),
his interest in work and his entelechy one of work accomplished (nitthita-
kammanta), and it may not be overlooked that these expressions are of
more than exclusively secular significance, the last, for example, corresponding to the kata-karaniya of the Arhat formula.

carpenters and painters who regarded themselves as descendants of the archetypal All-worker (whose image they drew for me). At one time they were working for me at my own house, chiefly at the making of a painted chest for my own use.[29] They were to be paid at a day rate when the work was done; but far from trying to spin out the time, they were so much interested, so much involved in their work, that they insisted on being supplied with adequate light, so that they could go on working after dark.[30] There is your answer to the problem of overtime.[31] It is under these conditions, as Plato says, that *"more* will be done, and *better* done, and *more easily* than in any other way."

We adopted above a widely accepted rendering of Sanskrit *dharma* as "law" or "justice." Absolutely, *dharma* is the eternal substance on which all being rests, and as such a property and appellation of the diety who is "the sustainer" (*dhartr*) of every operation" (*karma*, as in *Rgveda* I.11.4), i.e., in his royal nature as King of kings and accordingly *Dharma = Rājā eminenter.* So what is natural and right is that which happens *dharmanas pari* or *dharmatas*, "normally"; it is, for example, thus "in order" that a father is begotten in his descendants (*Rgveda* VI.70.3). Relatively, one's *sva-dharma* (*sua justitia*) is the natural law of one's own being, and so at the same time one's "lot" and one's "duty," which is also one's own-task or vocation (*sva-karma*). Unquestionably then, a correspondence of functions to varieties of natural (natal) endowment in a human society is, from the Indian point of view, nothing arbitrary, but a reflection on earth of the immutable Justice by which all things are governed. Whoever may maintain that the caste system is in fact unjust must nevertheless allow that its primary purposes are just.

In this matter, as in so many others, there is a fundamental agreement of the Indian and Greek theories. For Plato, the cosmic, civic, and individual orders or "cities" are naturally governed by one and the same law of justice δικαιοσύνη [*dikaiosyné*]; and among the accepted senses of "just" is that of "civilized." What "justice " means is discussed at some length in the second and fourth books of the *Republic.* For Plato it is, of course obvious that "the same kinds γένος [*genos*], etymologically the Sanskrit *jāti*) equal in number are to be found in that state and in the soul"

---

[29] Now in the Colombo Museum.
[30] I once cited these facts in the course of a lecture given at one of our larger woman's colleges. I was informed that most of my audience found it almost incredible that men could thus ignore their own best economic interests; they could not imagine a willingness to work, unless for money.
[31] For those whose means of livelihood is also their natural vocation, the word has no meaning; their work is never done.

and that a city and a man are to be called just or unjust by the same standards, and he says that justice is realized "when each of the several parts of the community of powers performs its own task" (τὰ ἑαυτοῦ πράττει). Justice, he says, is the principle of doing what it is ours to do (τὸ τὰ ἑαυτοῦ πράττειν [to ta eautou pratteih] = sva-karma). Nothing will be more ruinous to the state than for the cobbler to attempt to do the carpenter's work, or for an artisan or money maker "led on by wealth or by command of votes or by his own strength to take upon himself the soldier's 'form' (εἶδος [eidos] = varna), or for a soldier to take upon himself that of a counsellor or warden, for which he is not fitted, or for one man to be a jack-of-all-trades"; and he says that wherever such perversions occur ,there is injustice. He points out that "our several natures ἑκάστου φύσις [physis] = sva bhāva) are not all alike, but different," and maintains that "everyone is bound to perform for the state one social service, that for which his nature is best adapted." And in this way "more will be produced, and of a better sort (or, more beautiful), and more easily, when each one does one work, according to his own nature, at the right time and being at leisure from other tasks." In other words, the operation of justice provides automatically for the satisfaction of all the real needs of a society.

In the light of this conception of justice we can better understand Matthew 6, 31, 33 where when men ask, What shall we eat and drink, and wherewith shall we be clothed? they are told: "Seek first the kingdom of God and his righteousness, and all these things shall be added unto you." For the word that here is rendered by "righteousness" the *Atharva Veda* employs the equivalent of that very δυκαιοσύνη [eikaiosyne] about which Plato has been talking; and it is evident that if we understand by God's righteousness, His *justice* as defined by Plato, to seek it first will mean that all other necessaries will be provided for—"for the administration διακοναί [diaconia] of this service λειτουργια [leitourgia] not only supplies the wants of the Saints, but is abundant also by many thanksgivings unto God" (II *Corinthians* 9, 12). That such are the real meanings of the texts is borne out by St. Paul's recommendation elsewhere to remain in that station of life in which we are, even when the higher call to the service of God has been heard. In the following quotation the italics are mine: "But as God hath distributed μεμέρικεν [memeriken] to every man, as the Lord hath called every one, so let him walk . . . Let *everyman abide in the same calling wherein he was called* . . .[32] For he that is called in the Lord, being a slave

---

[32] Like the corresponding. Skr. *vi-bhaj* (*Bhagavad Gita* IV. 13), implies the allotment of a due share or inheritance or "fate," the individuality that is

δοῦλος [*doulos*], is the Lord's freeman; likewise also he that is called, being free, is Christ's slave . . . Brethren, let every man wherein he is called, therein abide with God" (I *Corinthians* 7, 17-24). There is no incompatibility of human with divine service.

Plato's functional order takes account not only of the three "kinds" of free men in the state, which correspond to the three upper castes of the Indian system, but of another kind to which he refers as that of the "servants" διάκονι [*diakono*] comparable to the Indian *Sūdras* and men without caste. These are those "who in the things of the mind are not altogether worthy of our fellowship, but whose strength of body is sufficient for toil; so they, selling the use of this strength and calling the price "wages," are called "wage-earners" (*Rep.*, 371E). These are, of course, the "wage-slaves" of an industrial society, where they form a majority; those whose bodies are all they have to offer can only be described as slaves, if not, indeed, as prostitutes (cf. Aristotle, *Politics* 1254b18). Conversely, one who is legally a slave, but has far more than his mere physical strength to offer, is in no sense a prostitute, but a responsible individual with only political disadvantages: a good example of what I mean can be cited in Chrétien de Troyes' *Cligés*, where the faithful John is a master builder, who holds that he "ought to be burnt or hanged, were I to betray my lord or refuse to do his will." Or in Homer, where Odysseus' faithful swineherd and porter is anything but an irresponsible slave (Odyssey XVI.1, XVII.385).

In the Orient, where human relations count for more than money, the consensus of feeling rates slavery above wage-earning. For, as Aristotle says, "the slave is a partner in his master's life . . . there is a certain community of interest and friendship between slave and master in cases when they have been qualified by nature for these positions, although when they do not hold them in that way, but (only) by law and constraint of force, the reverse is true" (*Politics* 1255 b, 21; 1260 a 10); while where men, however nominally free, are merely hired until their services are no longer needed, there may be no community of interest or friendship at all.[33] We could develop

---

born "like a garden already planted and sown." That distribution or dispensation is "a wondrous easy task," because it is not an arbitrary appointment, but rather the operation of an infallible justice by which we receive what our nature demands (cf. *Laws* 904 and Heracleitos fr. 79). It must always be remembered that "all is offered, but each takes only what it can receive."

[33] "On peut chasser un mercenaire mais non un serviteur hereditaire. Donc pour récolter la tranquillité et un bon service, il faut user de tact et de bonnes manières. L'hérédité, loin de les mettre à la merci de leur maître,

this point at great length, but can only indicate here that modern conceptions of slavery (and in like manner of serfdom) are too exclusively based on our imagination of the lot of galley slaves in the Roman Empire and upon what has been seen of slavery in America where (not to mention the iniquities of the trade itself) the condition of the slave was that of a man not merely suffering legal disabilities but also of one exploited economically in the same way that the wage-slave is now exploited, although actually "free" to work or starve. From evidences such as these alone we cannot judge of any institution. In Persia, a colleague of mine engaged in excavation often received from the local Sheikh gifts of fruits and sweetmeats: one day he said to the messenger, "I suppose you are the Sheikh's servant?" and received the indignant answer, "No, sir! I am his *slave*." My reason for mentioning these things is to remind the student of institutions, and indeed all those who have to live in the modern world of enforced intimacy with people of all nations, that we must not be misled by the mere names of things, but ask ourselves whether, for example, "liberty" and "serfdom" are actually exactly what we had supposed them to be; what we are really concerned about is the human reality of the institutions, and that depends far more upon the people whose institutions they are than upon the looks of the institutions themselves. That is also the reason why we have to take so much account, not merely of the forms themselves, but of the idealogical background in which they are worked. It must be impossible to judge of the propriety of any social formula unless we have a knowledge of what is regarded as the main purpose of life in the society that we are examining. We are not defending slavery, or even the caste system as such, but merely pointing out that under normal circumstances slavery may be a far less oppressive institution than wage-slavery must always be, and that the caste system cannot be judged by concepts of success that govern life in a society organized for over-production and profit at any price, and where it is everyone's ambition to rise on the social ladder, rather than to realize his own perfection.

In one respect the vocational organization of Greek society seems at first sight to differ from that of India, viz., in that in Plato's time and later, the vocation is not necessarily hereditary, the situation in this respect being different in different communities (cf. Aristotle, *Politics* 1278 5). What this really means is that in Hellenistic Greece an older system in which vocational status had been hereditary and divinely sanctioned was breaking down, and as Hocart says, *"Nous avons ici un excellente exemple du processus appelé communément, sans qu'on sache exactement en quoi il consiste, sécularisation"* (p. 235). Secularization: a subtraction of meaning from form, a "sundering of soul from spirit" not in the scriptural sense but *à l'envers*, a materialization of all values. That is what factually takes place whenever a traditional culture is overwhelmed by those who believe that "progression in line with the manufacturing enterprise of civilization must be allowed free course" whatever the human consequences may be;[34] whenever those who maintain that "such knowledge as is not empirical is meaningless" assume the control of education; whenever hereditary services and loyalties are "commuted" for money payments, and become "rents," and classes of *rentiers* or shareholders are created whose only interest is in their "interest." I am well aware, of course, that the "scientific humanist," rationalist, economic determinist, and village atheist are agreed that religion, designed by cunning aristocrats and interested priests in order to secure their own privileged positions, has been "the people's poison"; we shall not argue here that religion has either a supernatural basis or is not a religion, but will say that in societies organized for moneymaking, *advertisement*, designed by cunning manufacturers to secure their own privileged status, is *really* the people's poison, and that that is only one of the many ways in which what is called a civilization has become "a curse to humanity." Has it ever occurred to those who attack the caste systems, which they regard as unjust, that there are also values, or that the liberal destroyer of institutions, the protestant and rebel, *ipso facto* makes himself responsible for the preservation of their *values?*

Let us conclude with a reference to only one of these values. We have seen that in India it is taken for granted that a man is in love with the work to which he is born and for which he is by nature fitted. It is even said that a man should rather die at his post than adopt another's vocation. That may have seemed extreme. But let us see what Plato thinks. He tells us that Aesculapius knew that for all well-governed peoples there is a work assigned to each man in the city which he must needs perform, and no one has leisure to be sick and doctor himself all his days. And this we see, absurdly enough in the craftsman's case, but not in that of the wealthy, and so-called blessed man. He points out that a carpenter,

---

place celui-ci entre leurs mains. Sparta conserva le servage sous un forme qui paraissait très rude aux Athéniens, mais leurs opinions ont à peu près autant de valeur que les opinions de nos libéraux sur la caste indienne et l'esclavage africain" (A. M. Hocart, *loc. cit.*, pp. 237-238).

[34] "Il a été également possible d'avilir les artisans grace a la machine . . . On a fait tomber de leurs mains la possibilité du chef d'oeuvre. On a effacé de leur âme le besoin de la qualité; on leur a donné le desir de la quantité et de la vitesse" (Jean Giono, *loc. cit.*, p. 67).

if he falls sick, will indeed consult a doctor, and follow his advice. But if anyone prescribes for him a long course of treatment with swathings about the head and other paraphernalia, he hastily says that he has no leisure to be sick, and that such a life of pre-occupation with sickness and neglect of the work that lies before him is not worth living. And is not the reason for this that the carpenter has a task and that life is *not* worth living upon condition of not doing his work? But the rich man has no such appointed task, the necessity of abstaining from which renders life intolerable" (*Republic* 406C-407A).

Suppose that in Western societies a rectification of existing economic injustices has taken place in the natural course of the progress of manufacturing enterprise, that poverty is no more, that all men are really "free," and everyone is provided with his television, radio, car (or autogyro), and icebox, and is always sure of good wages (or a dole). Under these circumstances, what is to make him work, even for all the shorter hours that will still be necessary if the necessaries of life are to be provided for everyone? In the absence of the "work or starve" imperative, will he not be inclined to take long holidays, or, it may be, to live on his wife's earnings? We know how difficult it is at the present day to adequately "regiment" the "lazy natives" of the savage lands that have not yet been so completely industrialized that a man must work for wages, or die. Suppose that men were really free to choose their work, and refused to undertake any such uncongenial tasks as, for example, mining, or refused to assume the burdens of public office? Might not a conscription of manpower be needed even in times of peace? That might be worse than the caste system looks even to be. I can see no other alternative to this situation but for a man to be so in love with the work for which he is naturally qualified that he would rather be doing this work than idling; no other alternative thon for the workman to be able to feel that in doing of what is his to do he is not only performing a social service and thereby earning a livelihood, but also serving God.